# SimpleChic

## *Designer Knits, SuperQuick!*

A MINNOWKNITS BOOK

Breckling Press

Library of Congress Cataloging-in-Publication Data

Eaton, Jil
    SimpleChic : designer knits, SuperQuick! / Jil Eaton.— 1st ed.
        p. cm.
        Includes bibliographical references and index.
        ISBN 0-9721218-1-1
        1.  Knitting—Patterns.  I. Title.


    TT820.E255 2003
    746.43'20432—dc21                          2003006501


This book was set in Neutraface by Bartko Design Inc.
Printed in Singapore

*Every effort has been made to be accurate and complete with all the information in this book. The publisher and the author cannot be responsible for differences in knitters' abilities, typographical errors, techniques, tools or conditions or any resulting damages or mistakes or losses.*

Editorial direction by Anne Knudsen
Cover and interior design by Kim Bartko, Bartko Design Inc.
Photography direction by Jil Eaton
Cover and interior photographs by Nina Fuller
Learn-to-knit illustrations by Joni Coniglio
Drawings by Jil Eaton
Schematics by Charlotte Parry
Technical writing and editing by Carla Scott, Judith Shangold, Charlotte Parry, and pattern checking by Janice Bye
Manufacturing direction by Pat Martin


Published by Breckling Press, a division of Knudsen, Inc.
283 Michigan Street
Elmhurst, IL 60126, USA

*To Nina Fuller . . .*

*. . . my extraordinary friend, a woman of myriad gifts, an individual full of creativity, integrity, intelligence, and charm. Nina and I have shared studios, raised our kids, laughed and cried, pushed each other to achieve more than we ever thought possible, and supported each other's endeavors, no matter the scope, budget, or schedule. Nina is enormously generous with her many talents, time, and energy. She has, since the very beginning of my business, captured every single shot in clear focus and gorgeous color, with inimitable style. I can not thank her enough.*

# Contents

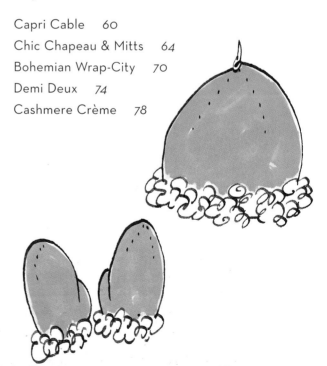

# A Word from Jil . . .

*SimpleChic* . . . a hat, a shell, perchance mittens or socks . . . no bit of yarn or imagination is ever wasted on such endeavors, and even true beginners can master these simple pieces. Quickly knit and instantly gratifying, such chic delights are simple enterprises, sometimes meaningful, never risky, but often transformative. Hats and mitts and socks and shawls warm not just our bodies but our hearts as well, and give reckless permission to all knitting addicts who fill basket after basket with whirlpools of color and fluff. Knit a hat or some socks for your sister or brother, your mom or your pop, and certainly a sweater for that brand-new baby. Knit with emotive abandon, whether your project is large or small, design to your heart's content, and enjoy this collection of light knitting fare. Remember, when we are knitting, all is right with the world.

*Jil Eaton*

Jil Eaton
Portland, Maine

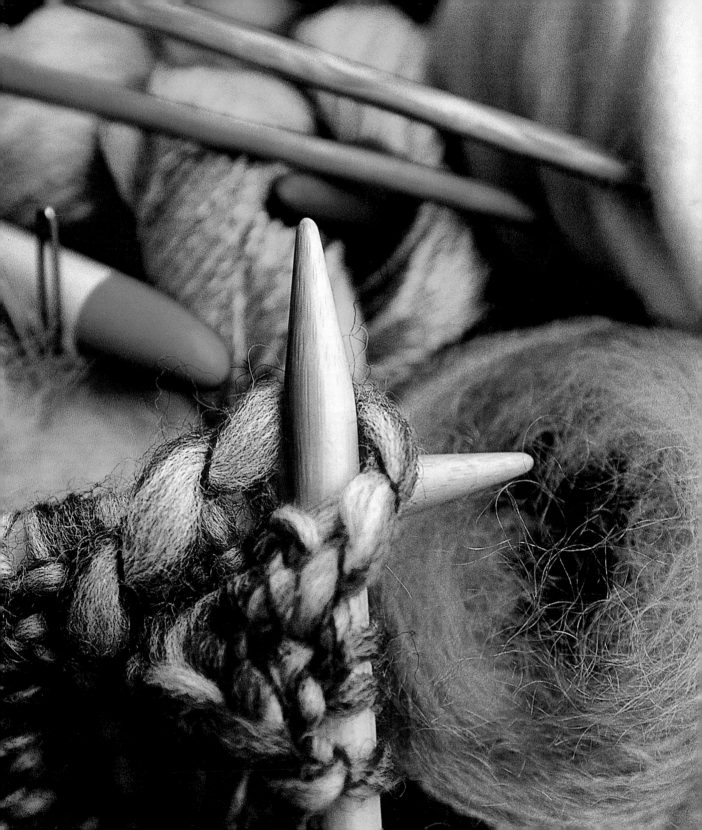

# Let's Knit!

Knitting as a practical endeavor is sometimes set aside these days, as we try to find time to accomplish our everyday necessities, and often beginning a complicated project is beyond our ken. But a hat! A neck-warmer or boot socks! Here we have the right-sized projects to give knitting a whirl, a jump-start for beginners or those returning to the craft. And just because something is quickly knit and simple to make doesn't preclude fashion or chic, as you'll find in this *SimpleChic* collection. Flirt with the myriad possibilities, pick up your needles and, before you know it, you'll be knitting away on some of these QuickKnit fashion tidbits.

*SimpleChic* is a collection of delectable projects for everyone. There are twenty chic and charming knits, some for babies, others for kids and adults. Cozy comfort prevails in hats and mittens, socks and scarves, with even a sweater or two. To delight the hound in your life, there's the enchanting Doggie Mac, too! Yarns are natural fibers and blends, in worsted to chunky weights, and in luscious color. Off-beat shapes and unusual combinations of color make each garment or accessory an uncommon knit,

wooly chic with flair. Most patterns are QuickKnits™ or SuperQuickKnits,™ perfect for even fledgling knitters, with a short knitting course to get you going.

Irresistible and inviting, each garment is photographed on location and is shot in exquisite detail. There are illustrations and schematics, too, so you can easily see the silhouette and shaping. As always, yardage is given both in English and metric. Each photograph tells you which yarns were used in the samples, allowing you flexibility as you make your own color decisions.

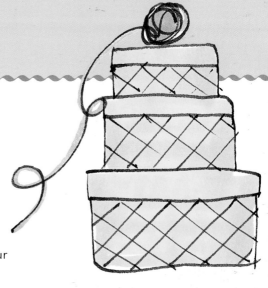

## A TISKET, A TASKET, A KNITTER'S BASKET!

I teach an assortment of classes, from beginner to advanced, but I recommend the same tools and books to all my students. These simple suggestions will quickly move you forward as you begin your knitting adventures. When we make it easy to do our work, success and contentment follow. This short collection of items will make you a happy knitter!

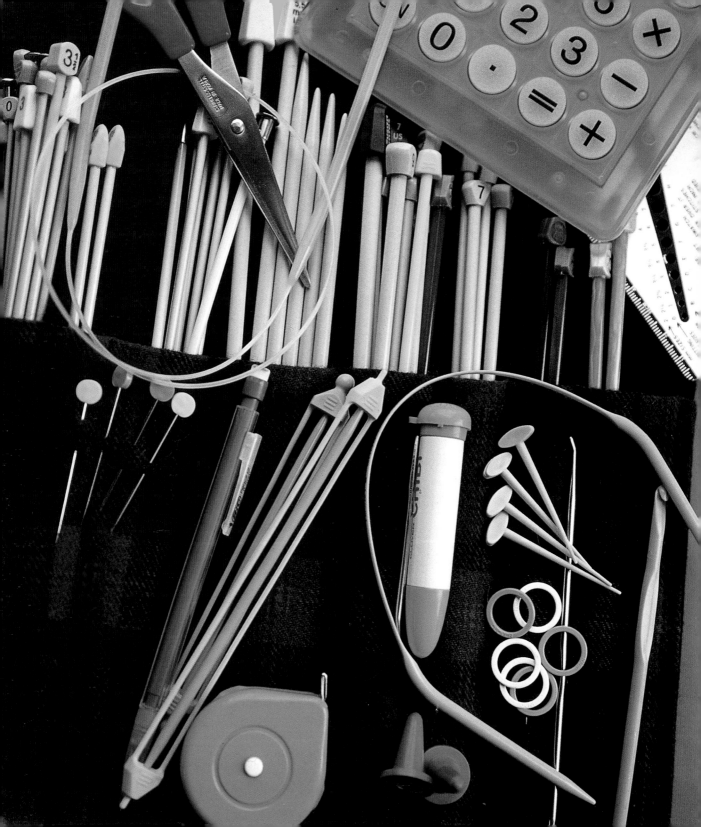

## QuickKnit Kit

Find a clear, zippered plastic case for the perfect knitting kit. A clear case allows you to see what's sieved to the bottom; you can usually find one in any cosmetics department. In your kit you should have the items listed below. If you set yourself up at the beginning with these items in your knitting kit, you have a portable studio, easily stashed in your knitting bag, as you change venues or projects.

- ☑ Small, very sharp scissors, used just for yarn

- ☑ Yarn needles: I like the Japanese Chibi needles with bent tips best

- ☑ Measuring tape: I like the retractable kind

- ☑ Yarn T-pins and yarn safety pins for marking or holding any dropped stitches

- ☑ Stitch holders, both long and short. English Aeros are my favorites

- ☑ Stitch markers: split-rings are good as they can be easily moved and removed

- ☑ Cable needle: I only use straight cable needles in various sizes

- ☑ Small calculator, which you will use constantly

- ☑ Point protectors, both large and small, to keep your work on the needles

- ☑ Needle/gauge ruler—essential!

- ☑ Crochet hooks: one large, one small

- ☑ "Dentists' tool" with one hooked end and one smooth end—invaluable! Check your favorite knitting Web site or catalog.

- ☑ Pen and small notebook

## CATCH-ALL BAG OR BASKET

I have dozens, one for each room of my house, several for traveling, and enormous versions for organizing the studio. I love lightweight mesh bags for travel, as the yarn can get heavy and baskets can be bulky. Use whatever carryall you like, but dedicate it to your projects and you'll always have everything at hand. I always have more than one project going at a time—to eliminate boredom as well as to provide projects for easy knitting and others for clear-headed progress.

### NEEDLES

You will, without doubt, want a complete set of needles, with doubles in your favorite sizes. I use different needles for various projects, depending on the yarn or garment.

### *Basic Needles*

Basic single-pointed needles are available in a variety of materials and in lengths from 9″ to 14″ (23 cm to 35.5 cm). I always use the shortest length needle possible, which puts less strain on my wrists.

## Circular Needles

You will want circulars for knitting-in-the-round as well as for large projects, where you use them as straight needles, working back and forth. Addi Turbo circular knitting needles are known as "amazing turbos," which is perfectly accurate! Made of nickel-plated brass that is easy on your hands, Addi needles actually speed up your knitting. The soft cords let stitches glide quickly along the needles, without snags or catches to slow you down, and the nickel plating makes a slick, effortless surface. Addi Turbo circulars easily accommodate any project, sized as they are from 12″ to 60″ (30 cm to 150 cm). They come in US size 00 to 36, easily accommodating any project. So smooth, so fast to work with, Addis are just a joy to have in your hands.

## Double-Pointed Needles

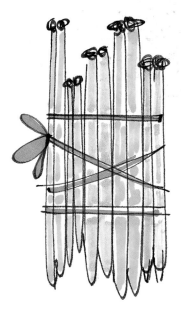

You use double-pointed needles, called dpns, for knitting-in-the-round. For projects requiring these pokey pointed sets, I generally use bamboo. They are as light as air, and stay put as you rotate your work, instead of shooting out as you move to the next needle. I always carry some in my knitting kit, too, for easy emergency repair and temporary stitch holders.

## NEEDLE CASES

If you begin using needle cases, your needles will be in one place, organized and accessible when you need them. Cases for both straight and circulars are readily available in knitting shops in a variety of styles and sizes. Whatever your preference, get some cases now, and get organized!

## KNITTING NOTEBOOK

All my students are required to have a knitting notebook, a three-ring binder used to organize patterns and projects. Clear three-ring pages that open at the top are perfect for individual projects and easily hold the pattern, any notes, and a small amount of the remaining yarn or the gauge swatch for reference. The yarn is also perfect for later repairs, and the notebook makes a keepsake diary of your projects. You'll be surprised how fast your projects mount up, and how much fun it is to remember the garments long after they've left your hands. You'll always have a little reminder of each in your notebook.

## Knitting Lights

If you can't see well you will have mistakes, guaranteed.
I have knitting lights placed in every room where I knit.
A high-intensity, but adjustable light will eliminate most
mistakes in your handwork, saving you from myriad
headaches.

## Yarn Winder

A table-mounted yarn winder is fabulous to have on
hand. They are found in your favorite knitting shop or
catalog and save a lot of time winding hanks of yarn (any
yarn that is not already wound in balls by machines). You'll
come to rely on your winder—unless, of course, you love
that yarn-winding ritual. I still have fond memories of
sitting at my mother's knee, swaying my hands back and
forth as she wound the yarn for a new project.

## YARNS, SOFT AND SUMPTUOUS

Remember, when you are doing hand work, you should always use the very best materials you can afford. You are often knitting heirlooms, gifts, or wonderful garments that will enjoy a long life, so you want the best. Try to avoid any notions of inexpensive man-made yarns; some of them can leach the oils from your hand. Others may have a tendency to "pill" or develop little bumps all over—not good. Worst of all, they do not provide comfort or warmth, and are usually available only in the most common colors. There are some new blends with naturals mixed with acrylics that are fine, but be careful and read the labels!

I love wool, for its warmth, elasticity, durability, and ability to hold beautiful dyes. Today's cottons are fabulous, and they faultlessly maintain shape and color. Cotton breathes and is comfortable in a great range of weather and climates. It is cool and durable, generally washable, perfect for long-wearing garments. The new blends and synthetic chenilles are fabulous, too. In this collection you will also find some new mixes and synthetics, which are quite delightful.

As always, my patterns are generic, with the required amounts for every garment given in yards and meters. You can easily substitute yarn colors, but be careful of

changing gauge weight. If the gauge is very different, as in a sport weight yarn rather than a bulky weight, you may find the garment looks entirely different. In a few instances, too, such as felted projects like Daisy Hat or Doggie Mac, I recommend you use the yarn specified or your results may vary.

I always give information on yarns that I have used for each knitted sample. This allows you to find the exact colors and weights. You might also want to experiment with colors, choosing your own creative palette. But again, *always* use the very best yarns you can afford, in natural fibers and blends.

## HOW TO MEASURE

Always measure the individual you are knitting for! This advice may seem simplistic, but I have found that often the easiest steps get overlooked. It is a simple matter to alter a pattern, making shorter or longer sleeves or bodice, and specific lengths make knitting easy. When you are knitting sleeves from the shoulder down, as I most often do, make any length adjustments in the bottom half of the sleeve. If the lucky individual being knit for is unavailable, measure a garment that fits that person comfortably. I recommend knitting a size up if the measurements fall between sizes, as a little big is infinitely better than too small and not wearable.

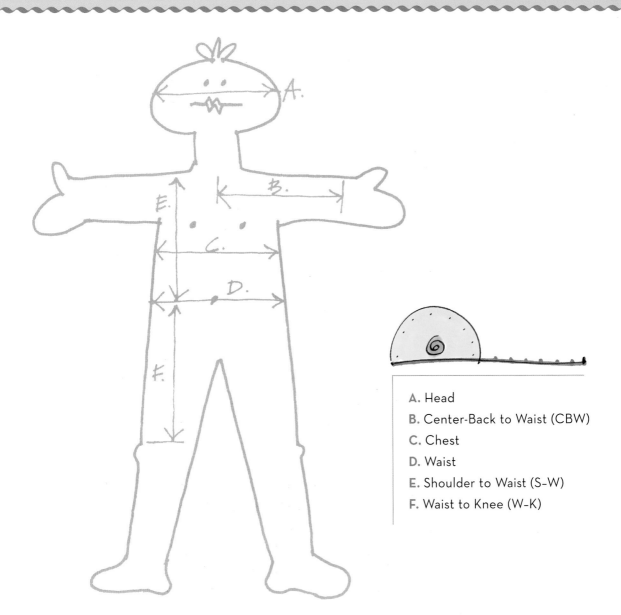

A. Head

B. Center-Back to Waist (CBW)

C. Chest

D. Waist

E. Shoulder to Waist (S–W)

F. Waist to Knee (W–K)

## KNIT TO FIT—EVERY TIME!

The single most important task when you are beginning a knitting project is to do a gauge swatch. The gauge swatch is a 4″ (10 cm) square, knit in the pattern called for and using the recommended needle size. *If you want your garments to fit, do your gauge swatch!* Period! Getting the correct gauge allows you to make a fabric that is even and smooth, with the correct drape and hand, never mind being the correct size. Even a hat that is off gauge one stitch per inch may be five inches too big or small, even with a bulky yarn!

As you progress with your knitting skills, you will find that knitting the gauge swatch is arguably the most creative part of the project, for this is where you make all your design decisions for each garment. My ideas are only a jumping-off point; you can go wild mixing and matching yarns, as long as you "get your gauge"! So please, please, please, just do it!

### MAKING A GAUGE SWATCH

A gauge swatch takes a very short time to knit but gives you all the information you need to knit a piece that will fit the way you want and expect. Your gauge swatch then becomes part of your knitting history, and gives you an

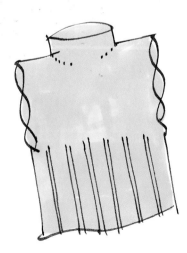

extra bit of yarn for emergencies. I know many of you skip your gauge swatch, especially for newborn projects. But getting the correct gauge will make all the difference in the success of your knitting.

Your gauge, or the correct number of stitches per inch or centimeter, and the correct number of rows called for in the pattern, is crucial to the success of your knitting project. For instance, knitting at even a half-stitch off gauge will make a significant difference in the final measurement of your garment. If the pattern calls for 100 stitches, at 5 stitches to the inch, and you are actually getting 5.5 stitches to the inch, your sweater will measure 18″ instead of 20″. Two inches is a big difference on any project, especially accessories and bulky knits.

Using the needles suggested in the pattern, cast on the correct number of stitches to make a 4″ (10 cm) swatch, plus 6 more stitches. Knit 3 rows. Always knit 3 stitches at the beginning and end of every row, and work straight in the pattern stitches called for until the piece measures 4″ (10 cm), then knit 3 rows and bind off. Lay the swatch on a flat, smooth surface. Measure inside the garter stitch frame; you should have an exact 4″ (10 cm) square. If your swatch is too big, or you have too few stitches per inch or centimeter, change to a needle

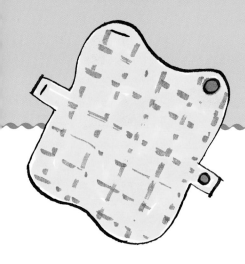

one size smaller. If your swatch is too small, or there are too many stitches per inch or centimeter, change to the next size larger needles. Changing one needle size either up or down at a time, keep knitting swatches until you achieve the correct gauge. The number of stitches per inch or centimeter is the most important; if the row gauge is eluding you, you can adjust as you work through the pattern.

I usually knit fast and loose, especially at the end of the day, and I always begin my swatching with needles one size smaller than those recommended in the pattern or on the yarn ball band. Always remember, these are *recommendations* only, as we all knit differently with various needles and yarns. Always do your gauge with the exact needles you will be using for the project, too . . . there can be a difference in gauge between plastic, metal, or bamboo needles on the same yarn! And check your gauge again after working about 4″ (10 cm), just to be sure you're still getting the gauge. Getting into the habit of doing your gauge swatch will fine tune your craftsmanship, making you a better knitter for life.

## ROW COUNTING

If you will count your rows, you will have a perfectly matching front and back, or two exactly matched sleeves. I always include row counts in my gauge section for every pattern, and you can always count based on the garment chart. If you stretch one piece to match another, the resulting pull will bother you when the garment is finished.

Count your rows vertically, beginning from the stitch on the needle and going down, always with the right side facing. If you constantly lose track of how many rows you have knitted, try getting into the habit making tally marks in your notebook.

My motto—when in doubt, tear it out—applies every time any of my knitting is less than perfect. So count your rows for perfect results and easy finishing.

## FINISH UP!

Finishing the knitting is one thing, but putting actual garments together is another separate and tricky task, requiring rested concentration and clear attention to detail.

Finish in the morning, in good light, and on a flat surface. Good finishing means the difference between a beautiful piece and a mediocre effort, so wait until you're fresh and able, and avoid the "happy hands at home" effect.

I usually design sweaters with sleeves knit from the shoulder down, using a knitted shoulder seam bind-off, with the seam on the exterior. This technique is worked with wrong sides facing, which results in a neat seam on the outside of the shoulder ridge, a little design detail. This seam finishing gives the shoulder stability, as well as being a fashion statement. Then you only have to sew sleeve and side seams to finish, and voilà, you're done!

## HOW TO BLOCK

When your knitting is complete, or when you have finished a garment piece, weave in all the loose tails of yarn on each piece. In fact, when I'm adding colors or the next ball of yarn, I always leave a 6" (15 cm) length, which makes the weaving-in at the end much easier. I think keeping your knitting neat has a payoff, so I tend to weave in ends sooner rather than later. Cover each piece with two damp towels, one under and one over, pinning the pieces in place. Alternatively, you can pin them to a blocking board, a wonderful invention that is available through catalog and yarn shops. Lightly steam at the appropriate setting for the yarn you are using, and dry your garment flat on a towel, mesh rack, or the blocking board/table if you have one. Blocking usually improves the look of your garment, as long as it is gently done, without mashing down the fibers. Be gentle. Many times I do not block at all, which results in a fresh and lively look.

## How to Launder Knits

Gauge swatches are absolutely perfect for testing the washability of a specific yarn, following the yarn label instructions. In fact, most yarns are machine washable, if you use a very gentle cycle and tepid water. Simply put the finished pieces in a small mesh bag. This holds their shape and gets them really clean. For wool, you should also use a no-rinse sweater soap such as Eucalan, which is available at fine yarn shops as well as on the Internet. Fill your washer with tepid (not cold) water, and add the laundry product. Soak the garment for 10 minutes; then go *directly* to the spin cycle *without* any rinsing, spin, remove and block as usual. You will save money on your dry cleaning, as well as wear and tear on your sweaters. You can use this technique for all your knitting garments. Take care of your hand-knits, and they will take care of you for a long, long time!

# An Old Yarn to

No one really knows when or where knitting originated. The best we can guess is that people began working with loops of fiber and discovered that they could make a strong and yet wildly flexible fabric by continuing the looping process. Knitting in its present day form first appeared in the Mediterranean around 1200 AD. Merchant fleets spread the craft throughout Europe and to the rest of the world.

The earliest pieces—usually found in tombs and churches—were worked in-the-round, using two colors, with designs ranging from simple geometrics to intricate patterns . . . socks in Egypt, liturgical gloves in Europe, finely knitted bags in Switzerland used, it seems, for holding relics, and pillows from Spanish tombs. Renaissance paintings even show the Virgin Mary knitting, working in-the-round on four needles, as we still do today!

## Guilds for Guys Only . . .

Knitting guilds during the Renaissance were very different from our groups today—for one thing, they were exclusively male! To be admitted, knitters trained rigorously, knitting full time for up to six years—more time than it takes to become

# Tickle the Fancy . . .

a doctor now! A Master knitter was required to knit many intricate garments, and even an amazingly elaborate carpet.

## Stockings and More Stockings . . .

Knitted stockings—so much more flexible than cloth hose with their cumbersome seams—never waned in popularity. In the 1500s, when short, full pantaloons became the fashion of the day, fancy knitted stockings allowed European gentlemen to show off their shapely legs! Later still, a lady-in-waiting presented the young Queen Victoria with her first pair of knitted black silk stockings. Her Majesty was enchanted and wore them exclusively to her dying day.

As time rolled on, knitting needles—once scarce and quite precious—finally became readily available in uniform sizes, a great boon for the craft. Knitting was easy to learn and carry and in time everyone began to knit items that could be sold. Socks, once again, were the knit garment of choice. The entire family would knit—even as they walked to the markets. In both Scandinavia and Africa, devices were designed to hold balls of yarn comfortably attached to the belt or waist, to knit and walk.

Yarns became available in higher quantity and quality during the 1800s, including new cotton yarns and wonderful wools from Merino sheep, still favorites today. And as knitting machines became common, hand knitting became a leisure-class craft. Patterns were printed at this time, and hand-knits were everywhere.

## In Praise of Plenitude!

As knitting wound its way around the world, individual knitters adapted it with their own styles and traditions and designs. Swedish women made rich, two-color sleeves to be sewn into their short-waisted woven jackets for pregnancy. Austrian women made complex vests for their men. South American Indians made caps and stockings. Russians and Lithuanians became known for their many-splendored mittens. Aran islanders knit complex cabled patterns in heavy-weight yarns for insulation and flexibility. Shetlanders knit the first lace shawls. Fishermen's sweaters, from Guernsey in the British Isles, were knit entirely in-the-round with densely patterned surfaces. The sleeves were knit from the shoulder down, so they could be re-knit as the elbows wore out. Families and villages developed their own specific patterns, so lost-at-sea fisherman could be identified by their sweaters.

The children of American settlers leaned to knit in school, making mittens and socks. Women in Great Britain and America knit for the war effort. Missionaries took knitting to India, which became famous for certain regional stockings. And although Japan has no knitting history of its own, missionaries brought the craft there and today Japanese techniques are some of the finest in the world. If you have the chance to study with a Japanese knitting master it is well worth your time, as the techniques are beautiful and unusual, especially those used for casting on and finishing.

## With a Little Bit of Love . . .

Hand-knitting has had its ups and downs and today it provides a welcome respite in our techno-driven society—a much needed creative outlet. Now mothers and grandmothers knit for their babies, while high-fashion designers like Karl Lagerfeld, Jean Paul Gaultier, and Calvin Klein incorporate hand-knits into their collections. Throughout history many great women, from queens to first ladies, like Eleanor Roosevelt, have knit up a storm, often turning to knitting in times of stress or hardship, as many of us do today. Through all, knits are made to be cherished, for whether we knit for peace or pleasure, joy or comfort, we always knit for love—love of yarns and color, texture and beauty, and love of giving. I hope you will add to this ancient tradition—just pick up your needles and knit!

# Knit One, Purl One, Magnifique!

I've always found that knitting gives us a productive way to relax, all the while creating unique fashions. Accessories and simple garments are the best for beginners—and for returning knitters—as the time element is greatly reduced. For instance, a child's or adult hat can be whipped up in a few hours, and even the sweaters in this collection are QuickKnits or SuperQuickKnits. The Elf Cap can be knit easily in a weekend, perfect for that last minute baby shower gift! So often I hear that you would love to knit, but don't have the time, energy, and dexterity, or whatever . . . just pick up some needles and give it a go. I think you'll be surprised how easy and rewarding it is!

This learn-to-knit section takes you through the basic skills of knitting, with drawings to help get you going. Although knitters have devised many clever methods of their own, I have included just two types of cast-ons, the *knit-on cast-on* and the *cable cast-on*. Once you have mastered the first method, you have actually learned the basic knit stitch. The cable cast-on is another variation and is used to form a sturdy yet elastic edge.

## MAKING A SLIP KNOT

**1.** Hold the yarn in your left hand, leaving a short length free. Wrap the yarn from the skein into a circle and bring the yarn from below and up through the center of the circle. Insert the needle under this strand as shown.

**2.** Pull on both the short and long ends to tighten the knot on the needle.

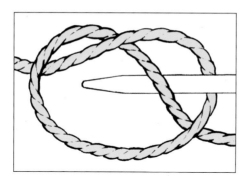

**STEP 1.** Slip Knot

**STEP 2.** Slip Knot

## KNIT-ON CAST ON

**1.** Hold the needle with the slip knot in the left hand and the empty needle in the right hand. Insert the right needle from front to back under the left needle and through the stitch. With the yarn in the right hand, wrap the yarn around the right needle as shown.

**2.** With the tip of the right needle, pull the wrap through the stitch on the left needle and bring to the front.

**3.** Slip the new stitch off of the left needle and onto the right needle. Repeat steps 1 to 3 for a simple knit-on cast-on. (For an alternate, more advanced method, continue on to step 4.)

**4.** Insert the right needle between the first two stitches on left needle and wrap the yarn around the needle as shown. Repeat steps 2 to 4 for the cable cast-on.

STEP 1. Cast on

STEP 2. Cast on

STEP 3. Cast on

STEP 4. Cast on

## MAKING THE BASIC KNIT STITCH

**1.** Hold the needle with the cast-on stitches in the left hand and hold the empty needle in the right hand. Insert the right needle from front to back into the first stitch on the left needle and wrap the yarn just as in the first step of the cast-on.

**2.** With the tip of the right needle, pull the wrap through the stitch on the left needle and onto the right needle. Drop the stitch from the left needle. A new stitch is made on the right needle. Repeat steps 1 and 2 until all the stitches from the left needle are on the right needle. Turn the work and hold the needle with the new stitches in the left hand and continue knitting back and forth.

**STEP 1.** Basic knit stitch

**STEP 2.** Basic knit stitch

## MAKING THE BASIC PURL STITCH

The purl stitch is basically the opposite of the knit stitch. Instead of pulling the wrapped yarn towards you, you will push it through the back of the stitch. Because it is harder to see what you are doing, the purl stitch is a bit harder to learn than the knit stitch. When you knit one row, then purl one row, you create the stockinette stitch.

1. Hold the needle with the cast-on stitches in the left hand, and hold the empty needle in the right hand. Insert the right needle from back to front, into the first stitch on the left needle, and wrap the yarn counter clockwise around the needle as shown.

2. With the tip of the right needle, pull the wrap through the stitch on the left needle and onto the right needle, as in the knit stitch. Drop the stitch from the left needle. A new stitch is made on the right needle. Continue in this way across the row.

Basic purl stitch

## STOCKINETTE STITCH

On straight needles, knit on the right side, purl on the wrong side. On a circular needle, knit every row.

## GARTER STITCH

When knitting with straight needles, knit every row. On a circular needle, knit one row, purl one row.

## DECREASE OR KNIT 2 TOGETHER (K2TOG)

Hold the needle with the knitted fabric in the left hand and hold the empty needle in the right hand. Insert the right needle from front to back through the first two stitches on the left needle. Wrap the yarn and pull through the two stitches as if knitting. Drop the two stitches from the left needle. One new stitch is made from two stitches; therefore one stitch is decreased.

Knit 2 together

## INCREASE

The most common way to increase is to knit in the front of the stitch, and, without removing the stitch from the left hand needle, knit in the back of the same stitch, and then drop the stitches from the left needle. This makes two stitches in one stitch.

## HOW TO BIND OFF

Hold the needle with the knitting in the left hand and hold the empty needle in the right hand. Knit the first two stitches. *With the left needle in front of the right needle, insert the tip of the left needle into the second stitch on the right needle and pull it over the first stitch and off the right needle. One stitch has been bound off. Knit the next stitch, then repeat from * until all the stitches are bound off.

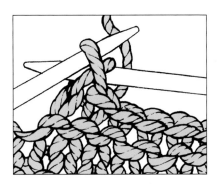

Bind off

# Rainy Days & Mondays

*Rain-proof hats, sox, and more to chase the clouds away*

Rainy days are perfect for gathering up your wool and needles, cozying down beside the fire, and knitting up a storm! These QuickKnit and SuperQuickKnit charmers are a wonderful way to while away the hours . . . whip up a Tippet scarf to stave off the cold, or maybe try the classic-chic Weekend Pullover for that tough-to-please teen. And the felted Daisy Hats are even waterproof!

# Tippet

*This short, flirty scarf with its tiny pompom trim is a chic and charming way to ward off the winter's chill. Pretty and oh, so simple, this short-stop knit will show you how to change colors and make pom poms! Use the very best yarn you can—cashmere is my recommendation . . .*

## SIZE

One size fits all

*Finished measurement:* 7" × 30" / 18 cm × 76 cm

## YARN ETC

*Aran weight yarn:* Approx 90 yd / 80 m in color A

Approx 90 yd / 80 m in color B

*Needles:* Size 9 US (5.5 mm), size 5 UK, or size needed to obtain gauge

*Sample in photograph knit in Classic Elite's Lavish Cashmere, Blue #92560 and Brown #92557*

## GAUGE

16 sts and 22 rows = 4" / 10 cm in pat

*Always check gauge to save time and ensure correct yardage and correct fit!*

### Ridge Pattern

Rows 1, 3, and 5 (RS): k

Rows 2 and 4: p

Rows 6, 8, and 10: k

Rows 7 and 9: p

Repeat rows 1 to 10 for ridge pattern

## SCARF

With A, cast on 28 sts. Work nine repeats of ridge pat, then work rows 1 to 5 again. **Next row:** Change to B and cont in ridge pat, working rows 6 to 10. Work nine more repeats. Bind off.

## FINISHING

Make eleven pompoms each from A and B as follows: Wind yarn around two fingers about 15 times. Cut yarn and remove from fingers. Tie a 12" / 30 cm piece of yarn tightly around middle of pompom. Cut loops and trim ends so that pompom measures ½" / 1.25 cm in diameter. Sew to each end of scarf, alternating one of color A with one of color B.

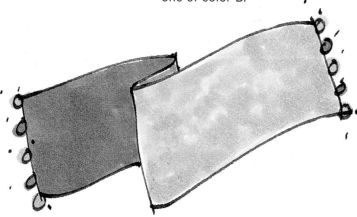

# Weekend Pullover

This SuperQuickKnit pullover is designed to be unisex. It will stop you from stealing your boyfriend's sweater—unless, of course, you make it for him! The super-bulky yarn and big needles make quick work of this surprisingly simple project, which sports V-neck shaping without any further finishing or trim.

## SIZES

*Finished chest:* 40 (45 - 48 - 53 - 56)" / 102 (114 - 122 - 135 - 142) cm

*Finished length:* 25 (26 - 27 - 28 - 29)" / 63.5 (66 - 68.5 - 71 - 73.5) cm

## YARN ETC

*Super-bulky weight yarn:* Approx 625 (725 - 800 - 925 - 1000) yd / 575 (665 - 735 - 850 - 920) m

*Needles:* Size 13 US (9 mm), size 00 UK, or size needed to obtain gauge

*Double-pointed needles (dpns):* Size 13 US (9 mm), size 00 UK

Stitch holders

*Sample in photograph knit in Jaeger's Natural Fleece #524*

## GAUGE

10 sts and 15 rows = 4" / 10 cm in St st

Always check gauge to save time and ensure correct yardage and correct fit!

## BACK

Cast on 50 (56 - 60 - 66 - 70) sts. Work in St st until piece measures 25 (26 - 27 - 28 - 29)″ / 63.5 (66 - 68.5 - 71 - 73.5) cm from beg or desired length to shoulder, ending with a RS row. **Shape shoulders:** Work 16 (19 - 20 - 23 - 24) sts and place on holder for shoulder, bind off 14 (18 - 20 - 20 - 22) sts for neck, work rem sts and place on holder for other shoulder.

## FRONT

Work as for back until piece measures 20 (21 - 22 - 23 - 24)″ / 51 (53.5 - 56 - 58.5 - 61) cm from beg or 5″ / 12.5 cm less than length of back. Mark center of work. **Shape neck, next row (RS):** Work to 4 sts before center, sl 1, k2tog, psso, k1; join another ball of yarn, k1, k3tog, k rem sts. Working both sides with separate balls of yarn, p next row. Rep last two rows 0 (0 - 1 - 1 - 2) times more—23 (26 - 26 - 29 - 29) sts rem each side. **Next row (RS):** Work to last 3 sts before neck, sl 1, k1, psso, k1; with other ball, k1, k2tog, k rem sts. P next row. Work last two rows 6 (6 - 5 - 5 - 4) times more—16 (19 - 20 - 23 - 24) sts rem each side.

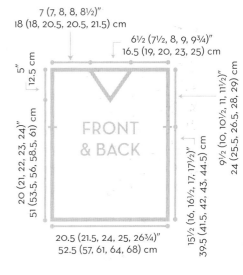

7 (7, 8, 8, 8½)″
18 (18, 20.5, 20.5, 21.5) cm

6½ (7½, 8, 9, 9¾)″
16.5 (19, 20, 23, 25) cm

5″
12.5 cm

9½ (10, 10½, 11, 11½)″
24 (25.5, 26.5, 28, 29) cm

20 (21, 22, 23, 24)″
51 (53.5, 56, 58.5, 61) cm

FRONT & BACK

15½ (16, 16½, 17, 17½)″
39.5 (41.5, 42, 43, 44.5) cm

20.5 (21.5, 24, 25, 26¾)″
52.5 (57, 61, 64, 68) cm

Work even until front measures same as back to shoulder, ending with a WS row. Place sts for shoulders on holders.

## SHOULDER SEAMS

For each shoulder, k seam tog as foll: sl front and back shoulder sts from holders to two dpns. Hold pieces together with *wrong sides* facing each other and sweater front facing you. With a third dpn, k first st from front needle tog with first st from back needle, *k next st from front and back needles tog, sl first st over second st to bind off; rep from * until all sts are bound off. Cut yarn and pull end through loop.

## SLEEVES

Place markers on front and back for armholes 9½ (10 - 10½ - 11 - 11½)" / 24 (25.5 - 26.5 - 28 - 29) cm down from shoulder seams. With RS facing pick up and k48 (50 - 52 - 56 - 58) sts between markers. Starting with a p row, work five rows in St st. Dec one st each edge on next row, then every sixth row 8 (8 - 6 - 4 - 2) times more, then every fourth row 4 (4 - 7 - 10 - 13) times—22 (24 - 24 - 26 - 26) sts rem. Work even until sleeve measures 19 (20 - 21 - 21½ - 22)" /

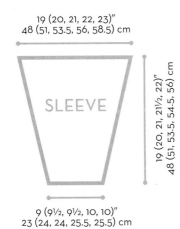

19 (20, 21, 22, 23)"
48 (51, 53.5, 56, 58.5) cm

SLEEVE

19 (20, 21, 21½, 22)"
48 (51, 53.5, 54.5, 56) cm

9 (9½, 9½, 10, 10)"
23 (24, 24, 25.5, 25.5) cm

48 (51 - 53.5 - 54.5 - 56) cm or desired length. End WS row.
Bind off knitwise.

## FINISHING

Sew side and sleeve seams.

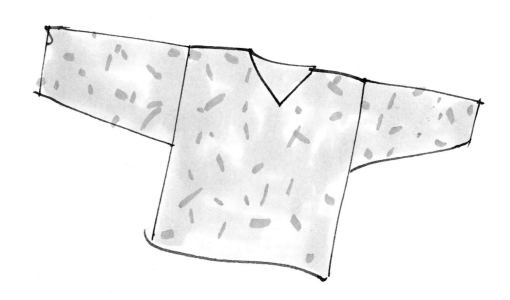

# Daisy Hat

Warm and waterproof, this jaunty pillbox hat is fit for the Easter parade. You'll knit in-the-round using four needles and learn an easy felting technique. Do use the Brown Sheep Bulky yarn specified—it felts beautifully. Differences in washing machines and water temperatures can affect felting; check your project after each washing.

## SIZES

Child (adult)
Finished size with I-cord edging, before felting: Approx 26 (29)" / 66 (73.5) cm
Finished size after felting: Approx 20 (22)" / 51 (56) cm

## YARN ETC

Bulky weight wool: Approx 110 (125) yards / 100 (115) m
1 set (five) double-pointed needles (dpns): Size 11 US (8 mm), size 0 UK, or size needed to obtain gauge
Circular needle: 16" or 20" (40 cm or 50 cm) length, size 11 US (8 mm), size 0 UK
Four buttons: 1½" / 4 cm
Square of felt: 6" / 15 cm
Sample in photograph knit in Brown Sheep Bulky #M110
Buttons from www. zecca.net

## GAUGE

Before felting: 10 sts and 16 rows = 4" / 10 cm in St st
After felting: 14 sts and 28 rows = 4" / 10 cm

Always check gauge to save time and ensure correct yardage and correct fit!

47

## Hat

Cast on 4 sts to one dpn. Inc 1 st in each st on next row—8 sts. Divide sts evenly over four dpns (2 sts on each needle). Join, being careful not to twist sts, and working in rnds of St st (k every rnd), inc 1 st at end of each needle every rnd (therefore 4 sts increased every rnd) until there are 72 (80) sts, or 18 (20) sts on each needle. For turning ridge, k one rnd, p two rnds. Cont to k every rnd for 4 (5)″ / 10 (12.5) cm, or desired depth. Transfer sts to circular needle.

## I-Cord Border

With two dpns, cast on 4 sts. **Row 1:** k4, do not turn work, but slide sts to other end of needle. **Row 2:** k3, pulling first st tightly, and k last st tog with first st from circular needle through back loop; slide sts to other end of needle. Rep rows 1 and 2 until all sts from hat are used. Bind off. Sew ends of I-cord tog.

## FELTING

Due to temperature fluctuations, felting time will vary. Check often for sizing. In washing machine, set on hot wash/cold rinse for a small load, place hat in water with 1 tsp of dishwashing liquid detergent, and run through longest cycle. Check size, then run through again if necessary. Remove, shape hat, and let dry.

## DAISY APPLIQUES

Trace daisy shape and cut out. Pin to felt square and cut around shape. Sew daisies and buttons around hat.

## Notes

- The finished size of a felted hat can be affected by the type of yarn you are using as well as the temperature of water in your washing machine. The measurements here are consequently approximate, and it may require some extra experimentation to achieve the desired size.

- Different yarns and colors may felt more or less, making a smaller or larger hat and thus may require different amounts of yarn to achieve the desired size. For best results, use a single ply, roving type yarn.

# Bow Cardi

*The perfect party sweater for Park Avenue tea or Thanksgiving dinner! And the bow is simply chic, pulled through the belt loops and tied to perfection. Different ribbons can change the look entirely. The pretty I-cord trim is an easy but beautiful way to finish edges.*

## SIZES

Child: 2 (3 - 4)
*Finished chest:* 27 (28 - 30)" / 67 (71 - 75) cm
*Finished length:* 12½ (13½ - 14½)" / 32 (34.5 - 37) cm

## YARN ETC

*Mohair or novelty yarn to obtain gauge below:* Approx 250 (300 - 350) yd / 230 (275 - 320) m
*Needles:* Size 9 US (5.5 mm), size 5 UK, or size needed to obtain gauge
*Double-pointed needles (dpns):* Size 9 US (5.5 mm), size 5 UK
*Crochet hook:* Size H US (5 mm), size 6 UK
Stitch holders
*Ribbon:* 4" × 60" / 10 cm × 152 cm
*Sample in photograph knit in Berroco's Mohair Classic, Lime #B1485*

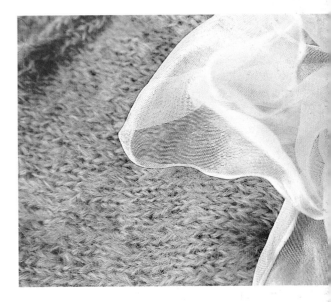

## GAUGE

16 sts and 20 rows = 4" / 10 cm in St st

*Always check gauge to save time and ensure correct yardage and correct fit!*

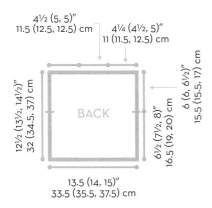

4½ (5, 5)"
11.5 (12.5, 12.5) cm

4¼ (4½, 5)"
11 (11.5, 12.5) cm

12½ (13½, 14½)"
32 (34.5. 37) cm

BACK

6 (6, 6½)"
15.5 (15.5, 17) cm

6½ (7½, 8)"
16.5 (19, 20) cm

13.5 (14, 15)"
33.5 (35.5, 37.5) cm

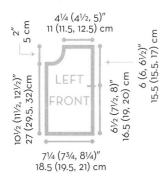

2"
5 cm

4¼ (4½, 5)"
11 (11.5, 12.5) cm

10½ (11½, 12½)"
27 (29.5, 32) cm

LEFT FRONT

6 (6, 6½)"
15.5 (15.5, 17) cm

6½ (7½, 8)"
16.5 (19, 20) cm

7¼ (7¾, 8¼)"
18.5 (19.5, 21) cm

## BACK

Cast on 52 (56 - 60) sts. Work in St st until piece measures 12½ (13½ - 14½)" / 32 (34.5 - 37) cm or desired length to shoulder, ending with a WS row. Work 17 (18 - 20) sts and place on holder for right shoulder. Bind off 18 (20 - 20) sts for neck. Work rem sts and place on holder for left shoulder.

## LEFT FRONT

Cast on 29 (31 - 33) sts. Work in St st until piece measures 10½ (11½ - 12½)" / 27 (29.5 - 32) or 2" / 5 cm less than length of back; end with a RS row. **Shape neck, next row (WS):** Bind off 5 (6 - 6) sts, p rem sts. Cont to bind off at the beg of every WS row 3 sts once, 2 sts twice—17 (18 - 20) sts rem. Work even until piece measures same length as back to shoulder. Place sts on holder.

## RIGHT FRONT

Work as for left front until piece measures same as left front to neck; end with a WS row. **Shape neck, next row (RS):** Bind off 5 (6 - 6) sts, k rem sts. Cont to bind off at beg of every RS row as for left front. Work even until piece measures same length as back to shoulder. Place sts on holder.

## SHOULDER SEAMS

For each shoulder, k seam tog as foll: sl front and back shoulder sts from holders to two dpns. Hold pieces together with *wrong sides* facing each other and sweater front facing you. With a third dpn, k first st from front needle tog with first st from back needle, *k next st from front and back needles tog, sl first st over second st to bind off; rep from * until all sts are bound off. Cut yarn and pull end through loop.

## SLEEVES

Place markers on front and back for armholes 6 (6 - 6½)" / 15.5 (15.5 - 17) down from shoulder seams. With RS facing pick up and k48 (48 - 52) sts between markers. Starting with a p row, work five rows St st. Dec 1 st each edge next row, then every fourth row 5 (6 - 6) times more, then every second row 3 (2 - 4) times—30 sts rem. Work even until sleeve measures 8 (8½ - 9)" / 20 (21.5 - 23) cm. Bind off knitwise.

12 (12, 13)"
30 (30, 33) cm

SLEEVE

8 (8½, 9)"
20 (21.5, 23) cm

7½"
19 cm

## FINISHING

Sew side and sleeve seams.

## I-Cord Edging

With dpns, cast on 3 sts. **Next row:** k3, *do not turn work. Slide sts to other end of needle to work next row from RS and k3; rep from * until I-cord is long enough to fit along left front, back neck, and right front edges. Do not bind off. Starting with cast-on end, sew I-cord to left front, back neck, and right front edges, adjusting length if necessary. Bind off.

## Belt Loops (Make 2)

With crochet hook, make 3" / 7.5 cm chain. Attach at each side seam, placing top of loop just below sleeve. Thread ribbon through belt loops.

# Italiano

Stroll the streets of Gstaad in cozy comfort in this faux fur neck-warmer. If this is your first time knitting with a specialty yarn, this SuperQuickKnit makes it a breeze. There are many faux fur-type yarns on the market, so make sure the one you use is high quality and of the softest fibers.

## SIZE

One size fits all
*Finished size: 6" × 17" / 15 cm × 43 cm*

## YARN ETC

*Faux fur yarn:* Approx. 135 yd / 125 m (used doubled)
*Needles:* Size 9 US (5.5 mm), size 5 UK, or size needed to obtain gauge
*Sample in photograph knit in Lang Furore #0001, used doubled*

## GAUGE

14 sts = 4" / 10 cm in St st using two strands held tog

*Always check gauge to save time and ensure correct yardage and correct fit!*

## NECKWARMER

With two strands of yarn held tog, cast on 59 sts. Work in St st for 6" / 15 cm. Bind off loosely.

## FINISHING

Sew short ends tog.

# Oh So Chic!

## ... for the fashion set

Knitting has never been more fashionable, with the top international design set and absolutely everyone else making and wearing hand-knit chic. The garments in this group are la crème de la crème, a far cry from the homemade concepts of yesteryear. So knit up one of these delicious confections and make your own fashion statement!

# Capri Cable

*Picture yourself sipping cappuccino in a café in Capri, wearing this chic sleeveless shell. The cable gives a charming and unexpected finish to the armholes. This pattern shows you how to cable both right and left. The cable, done on seven stitches, is a basic cable pattern. It looks complicated, but couldn't be easier.*

## SIZES

*Finished chest:* 34 (35 - 36 - 38)" / 86 (90 - 92 - 96) cm
*Finished length:* 19 (20 - 21 - 22)" / 48 (50 - 53.5 - 56) cm

## YARN ETC

*Worsted-weight yarn:* Approx 500 (550 - 600 - 650) yd / 460 (505 - 550 - 595) m
*Needles:* Size 9 US (5.5 mm), size 5 UK, or size needed to obtain gauge
*Double-pointed needles (dpns):* Size 9 US (5.5 mm), size 5 UK
Cable needle (CN)
Stitch holders
*Sample in photograph knit in Rowan's All Seasons Cotton #197*

## GAUGE

18 sts and 24 rows = 4" / 10 cm in rib st
16 sts and 24 rows = 4" / 10 cm in St st

*Always check gauge to save time and ensure correct yardage and correct fit!*

## Note

Always pull the first and second stitches of each row firmly to maintain a smooth edge. Once you learn the cable technique you will enjoy working the cable every sixth row. Make sure you remember to reverse the cable on each side!

## BACK

Cast on 85 (89 - 93 - 97) sts. Work in rib st for 11½ (12 - 12½ - 13)" / 29 (30 - 32 - 33) cm, ending with a RS row. **Next row (WS):** p2, k1, p3, [p2tog, p2] 18 (19 - 20 - 21) times, k1, p3, k1, p2—67 (70 - 73 - 76) sts. **Next row:** Work right cable panel, work in St st over next 53 (56 - 59 - 62) sts, work left cable panel. Cont in pats as established until piece measures 19 (20 - 21 - 22)" / 48 (50 - 53.5 - 56) cm from beg, ending with a RS row. **Shape shoulders:** Work 15 (17 - 18 - 20) sts and place on a holder for shoulder, work next 37 (36 - 37 - 36) sts for neck, work rem sts and place on another holder for shoulder. Join yarn and cont in St st on neck sts for 2" / 5 cm. Bind off loosely.

## FRONT

Work same as back.

## FINISHING

For each shoulder, knit seam tog as follows: sl front and back shoulder sts from holders to two dpns. Hold pieces together with *wrong sides* facing each other and sweater

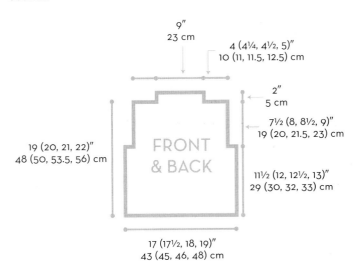

front facing you. With a third dpn, k first st from front needle tog with first st from back needle, *k next st from front and back needles tog, sl first st over second st to bind off; rep from * until all sts are bound off. Cut yarn and pull end through loop. Sew neck seams. Sew side seams.

9"
23 cm

4 (4¼, 4½, 5)"
10 (11, 11.5, 12.5) cm

2"
5 cm

7½ (8, 8½, 9)"
19 (20, 21.5, 23) cm

19 (20, 21, 22)"
48 (50, 53.5, 56) cm

FRONT
& BACK

11½ (12, 12½, 13)"
29 (30, 32, 33) cm

17 (17½, 18, 19)"
43 (45, 46, 48) cm

## Rib Stitch Pattern

Row 1 (RS): k2, *p1, k3; rep
  from *, end p1, k2
Row 2: k the knit sts and p the
  purl sts
Rep row 2 for rib st pattern

## Right Cable Panel
(over 7 sts)

Rows 1 and 3 (RS): k6, p1
Rows 2, 4, and 6: k1, p6
Row 5: sl 3 sts to CN and hold
  to back, k3, k3 from CN, p1
Rep rows 1 to 6 for right cable
  panel

## Left Cable Panel
(over 7 sts)

Rows 1 and 3 (RS): p1, k6
Rows 2, 4, and 6: p6, k1
Row 5: p1, sl 3 sts to CN and
  hold to front, k3, k3 from CN
Rep rows 1 to 6 for left cable
  panel

# Chic Chapeau & Mitts

*These warm wonders move from the streets of Paris to country estates with aplomb. Making this hat and mitten set will give you practice in five-needle knitting, the loop stitch, and making an I-cord trim. If you are a beginner, you could substitute a rolled edge trim instead of the loop stitch.*

## SIZES

Child (adult)

*Finished hat size: 19 (21)" / 48 (53.5) cm*

## YARN ETC

*For Hat*

*Worsted weight yarn: Approx 70 (85) yd / 65 (80) m in MC*

*Faux fur: Approx 80 (90) yd / 75 (85) m (use doubled)*

*For Mitts*

*Worsted weight yarn: Approx 85 (130) yd / 80 (120) m in MC*

*Faux fur: Approx 30 (35) yd / 28 (32) m (use doubled)*

*Needles: Size 8 US (5 mm), size 6 UK, or size needed to obtain gauge*

*Double-pointed needles (dpns): Size 8 US (5 mm), size 6 UK (hat only)*

Stitch holders and markers (mitts only)

*Sample in photograph knit in JCA / Reynolds Andean Alpaca Regal #6 and Berocco's Furz #3801 (double stranded)*

## GAUGE

18 sts and 24 rows = 4" / 10 cm in St st

12 sts and 12 rows = 4" / 10 cm in loop st with double stranded fur yarn

 *Always check gauge to save time and ensure correct yardage and correct fit!*

## HAT

With two dpns and MC, cast on 4 sts. Work I-cord top knot as foll: k4, *do not turn work. Slide sts to other end of needle to work next row from RS and k4; rep from * for 2½" / 6.5 cm. Inc 1 st in each st on next row—8 sts. Divide sts evenly over four dpns (2 sts on each needle). Join and k all rnds, inc 1 st at end of each needle every rnd (therefore 4 sts increased every rnd) until there are 88 (96) sts total or 22 (24) sts on each needle. Work even until piece measures 6½ (7½)" / 16.5 (19) cm from top knot. Bind off. (For a simple rolled rim, on next row, RS, dec 8 sts evenly across row. Continue in St st for 10 rows, then bind off.)

## BRIM

With a double strand of fur yarn, cast on 57 (73) sts. Work loop stitch as follows: **Row 1:** *k1, but leave st on left needle; bring yarn to front and wrap around thumb, bring yarn to back and k st again through back loop and sl both sts off needle; rep from * across. **Row 2:** p2 tog, across. Repeat rows 1 and 2 until band measures 1½ (2)" / 4 (5) cm. Bind off. Sew bound off edge of hat to bound off edge

### Note

If you are a beginner, you could simply do a rolled edge trim instead of the loop stitch until you have more experience. But I think many very simple garments are made extraordinary with small, interesting details. The loop stitch really is easy once you get the hang of it, and will add that *je ne sais quoi* to your project.

of brim so that when folded up, the loopy side of the brim faces out. Sew edges of brim tog.

## MITTS

With main color, cast on 28 (32) sts and work in St st for 2 (3)″ / 5 (7.5) cm, end with a WS row. **Next row (RS):** k, inc to 5 sts evenly across—33 (37) sts. Work even in St st for zero (four) rows. **Next row (WS):** p15 (17) sts, place marker (M), p 3 sts, place M, p rem sts. **Thumb gore, inc row:** k, inc in the st after the first M and before the second M. Cont in St st, working inc row every RS row until you have 11 (13) sts between markers, ending with a RS row.

### THUMB

**Next row (WS):** Work 15 (17) sts and place on holder, work 11 (13) thumb sts, work rem sts and place on holder. Cut yarn. Join yarn and cont to work thumb sts only for 1 (2)″ / 2.5 (5) cm, end WS row. **Next row:** k1, *k2tog; rep from * across, cut yarn, leaving long end and pull through rem sts. Sew thumb seam.

## HAND

With RS facing, k15 (17) sts from holder, pick up 3 sts across thumb, k rem sts from holder—33 (37) sts. Work even until mitten measures 6 (9½)" / 15 (24) cm from beg, end WS row. **Next row, dec row:** k1, *k2tog; rep from * across. **Next row:** p. Rep last 2 rows one more time. **Next row:** k1 (0), *k2tog; rep from * across—5 sts rem. Cut yarn leaving long end and pull through rem sts. Sew side seam.

## CUFFS

With a double strand of fur yarn, cast on 19 (25) sts. Work loop stitch as follows: **Row 1:** *k1, but leave st on left needle; bring yarn to front and wrap around thumb, bring yarn to back and k st again through back loop and sl both sts off needle; rep from * across. **Row 2:** p2tog, across. Repeat rows 1 and 2 a total of three times. Bind off. Sew cast on edge of cuff to cast on edge of mitt so that when folded back, the loopy side of the cuff faces out. Sew side seam.

# Bohemian Wrap-City

*Wrap yourself in this glamorous confection, perfect for the ballet, the opera, or downtown. The stole is knit in basketweave stitch, with an elegant embroidered bobble trim. Make sure you are generous with your bobbles, as they make the stole stylish. Simply put a length on a yarn needle, and bobble away.*

## SIZE

One size

*Finished stole:* 11½ " × 68" / 29 cm × 173 cm

## YARN ETC

*Mohair or novelty yarn that will knit to gauge below:* Approx 320 yd / 295 m in MC

Approx 25 yd / 23 m in CC

*Needles:* Size 10 US (6 mm), size 4 UK, or size needed to achieve gauge

Yarn needle

*Sample in photograph knit in Berroco's Mohair Classic #8222 and Monet # 3393*

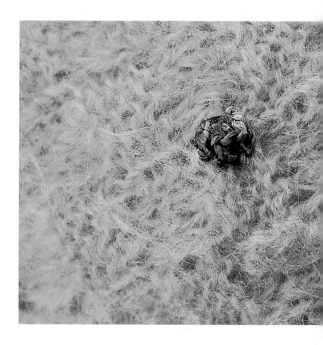

## GAUGE

14 sts and 20 rows = 4" / 10 cm in pat

*Always check gauge to save time and ensure correct yardage and correct fit!*

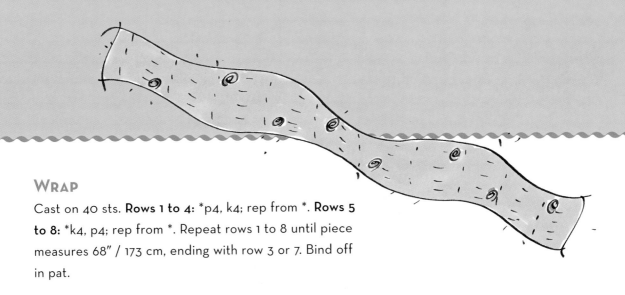

## WRAP

Cast on 40 sts. **Rows 1 to 4:** *p4, k4; rep from *. **Rows 5 to 8:** *k4, p4; rep from *. Repeat rows 1 to 8 until piece measures 68" / 173 cm, ending with row 3 or 7. Bind off in pat.

## BOBBLES

With CC, embroider eleven bobbles, placing first one 4" / 10 cm from bottom edge and 3" / 7.5 cm from side edge as follows: thread 24" / 61 cm piece of novelty yarn through yarn needle and double over. Go in and out of fabric, crisscrossing to make a small, round bobble that appears on both sides of the knitting. Cut yarn and secure end. Place ten more bobbles, spaced 6" / 15 cm apart and 3" / 7.5 in from left and right edges alternately (see diagram).

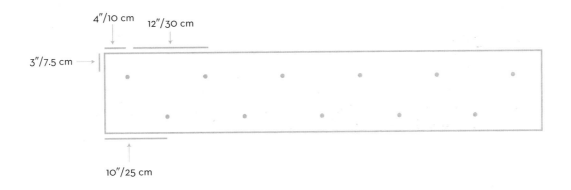

# Demi Deux

*Knit a hip, stylish warm-up for those brisk days before the deep chill. These easy-to-knit cables are a sure-fire way to add some style to even the simplest designs. The cozy neckwarmer and the half mitts both qualify as SuperQuick Knits!*

## SIZE

One size fits all
*Finished neckwarmer: 6″ × 18″ / 15 cm × 46 cm*

## YARN ETC

*For Mitts*
*Bulky weight wool to obtain gauge below:*
Approx 75 yd / 70 m
Stitch holders

*For Neckwarmer*
*Bulky weight wool to obtain gauge below:*
Approx 85 yd / 80 m
*Needles:* Size 10 US (6 mm), size 4 UK, or size needed to obtain gauge
*Circular needle:* 16″ / 40 cm length, size 10 US (6 mm), size 4 UK (neckwarmer only)
Cable needle (CN)
*Sample in photograph knit in Trendsetter's Dali, 100% Cashmere #187*

## GAUGE

14 sts = 4″ / 10 cm in St st

 *Always check gauge to save time and ensure correct yardage and correct fit!*

## DEMI MITTS

### RIGHT MITT

Cast on 26 sts. Work in St st and cable panel as foll: **Row 1 (WS):** p14, work row 1 of cable panel over next 10 sts, p2. Cont in St st and cable pat as established for 3" / 7.5 cm, ending with a RS row. **Next row (WS):** Work 14 sts, place marker (M), p3, place M, work rem sts.

### THUMB GORE

**Next row (RS), inc row:** Keeping to pat, inc in st after first M and before second M. Cont to work in pats as established, working inc row every RS row until there are 9 sts between markers, ending with a RS row. **Next row (WS):** Work 14 sts and place on a holder, p9 and leave on needle, work rem 9 sts and place on a holder. Cut yarn.

### THUMB

Join yarn and cont on thumb sts only as foll: cast on 1 st at beg of next two rows. Work even in St st for six more rows. Bind off. Sew thumb seam.

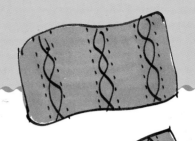

## HAND

Work sts from first holder, pick up and k3 sts across thumb gusset, work sts from second holder—26 sts. Cont in St st and cable pat until hand measures 2½ " / 6.5 cm above thumb, ending with a WS row. Bind off. Sew side seam.

## LEFT MITT

Cast on 26 sts and reverse pat as foll: **Row 1 (WS):** p2, work cable panel over next 10 sts, p14. Work as for right mitt for 3" / 7.5 cm, ending with a RS row. **Next row (WS):** keeping to pat, work 9 st, place M, p3, place M, work rem sts. Work thumb gore and complete as for right mitt.

# NECKWARMER

With circular needle, cast on 72 sts. Join, being careful not to twist sts, and put marker on needle to indicate beg of rnds. **All rnds:** k3, [work cable panel over 12 sts, k6] three times, work cable panel, k3. Work in pats as established until piece measures 6" / 15 cm. Bind off loosely and evenly in pat.

## Cable Panel
(over 12 sts)

Rnds 1, 2, 3, 5. 6, 7, and 8: p1, k1, p1, k6, p1, k1, p1

Rnd 4: p1, k1, p1, sl next 3 sts to CN and hold to back of work, k3, k3 from CN, p1, k1, p1

Rep rnds 1 to eight for cable panel

# Cashmere Crème

*Sumptuous and sophisticated, with its wide funnel neck, full fashioning, and set-in sleeves, Cashmere Crème is nonetheless simple to make. The bulky cashmere used in the sample photographed is so glorious the model wanted to learn to knit so she could whip it up herself. Do find such a soft and luxurious fiber for this high-fashion QuickKnit.*

## SIZES

*Finished chest:* 36 (40 - 44)" / 92 (102 - 112) cm
*Finished length:* 20 (20½ - 21)" / 51 (52 - 53.5) cm

## YARN ETC

*Bulky weight yarn:* Approx 600 (700 - 800) yd / 550 (640 - 735) m
*Needles:* Size 10.5 US (6.5 mm), size 3 UK, or size required to obtain gauge
*Circular needle:* 16" / 40 cm length, size 10.5 US (6.5 mm), size 3 UK
Stitch holders
*Sample in photograph knit in Classic Elite's Sinful cashmere #20093*

## GAUGE

12 sts and 18 rows = 4" / 10 cm in St st

*Always check gauge to save time and ensure correct yardage and correct fit!*

## BACK

Cast on 54 (60 - 66) sts. Work in St st until piece measures 12" / 30 cm or desired length to armhole, ending with a WS row. **Shape armhole:** Bind off 0 (0 - 2) sts beg of next two rows. **Next row (RS):** k2, sl 1, k1, psso, k to last 4 sts, k2tog, k2. **Next row:** p. Rep last two rows 5 (6 - 6) times more—42 (46 - 48) sts. Work even until armhole measures 7 (7½ - 8)" / 18 (19 - 20) cm, ending with a WS row. **Shape shoulders:** Bind off 4 (5 - 5) sts beg of next two rows, 5 sts beg of next two rows. Place rem 24 (26 - 28) sts on a holder for back neck.

## FRONT

Work same as back until armhole measures 3 (3½ - 4)" / 7.5 (9 - 10) cm, end WS row. **Shape neck, next row (RS):** Work 16 (17 - 17) sts, join second ball of yarn, work next 10 (12 - 14) sts and place on holder; work rem sts. Working both sides with separate balls of yarn, work dec row on next RS row as follows: Work to last 2 sts before neck, k2tog; with other ball, sl 1, k1, psso, k rem sts. **Next row:** p. Rep dec row next row * then on the fourth row, then on the second row; rep from * until 9 (10 - 10) sts rem. Work even until piece measures same length as back to

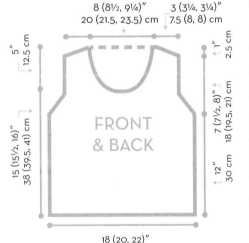

8 (8½, 9¼)"
20 (21.5, 23.5) cm

3 (3¼, 3¼)"
7.5 (8, 8) cm

5"
12.5 cm

1"
2.5 cm

FRONT
& BACK

7 (7½, 8)"
18 (19.5, 21) cm

15 (15½, 16)"
38 (39.5, 41) cm

12"
30 cm

18 (20, 22)"
46 (51, 56) cm

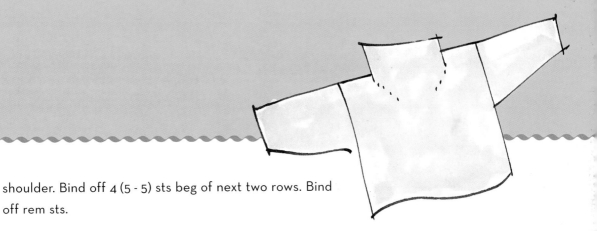

shoulder. Bind off 4 (5 - 5) sts beg of next two rows. Bind off rem sts.

## SLEEVES

Cast on 26 (28 - 30) sts and work in St st for 2″ / 5 cm, ending with a WS row. Inc 1 st each edge on next row, then every twelfth (eighth - eighth) row a total of 6 (9 - 9) times—38 (42 - 48) sts. Work even until piece measures 15 (16 - 17)″ / 38 (41 - 43) cm or desired length to armhole, ending with a WS row. **Shape cap:** Bind off 0 (0 - 2) sts at beg of next two rows. **Next row (RS):** k2, sl 1, k1, psso, k to last 4 sts, k2tog, k2. **Next row:** p. Rep last two rows 5 (6 - 6) times more—26 (28 - 30) sts. Bind off.

## FINISHING

Sew shoulder seams. **Collar:** With RS facing and circular needle, start at left shoulder seam and pick up and k21 sts along left neck edge, k sts from front holder; pick up 21 sts along right neck edge, k sts from back holder—76 (80 - 84) sts. Join and work in St st (k all rnds) for 7″ / 18 cm. Bind off loosely. Sew in sleeves, matching dec edges of sleeve cap with dec edges of armhole shaping. Sew side and sleeve seams.

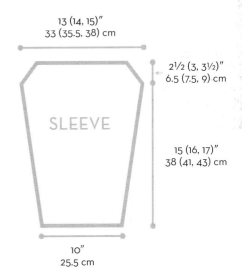

13 (14, 15)″
33 (35.5, 38) cm

2½ (3, 3½)″
6.5 (7.5, 9) cm

SLEEVE

15 (16, 17)″
38 (41, 43) cm

10″
25.5 cm

# BABES & PUPS

*Gems for teens and tots—*
*and puppy too!*

FROM COMFY CLOG SOCKS to zany chapeaux, you will find these projects a delight for young and old alike. Your pups will be especially pleased with this plaid all-weather coat, which will keep them warm and dry— never mind making them the most chic pooches on the block! All QuickKnits, all treasures, these are fun and satisfying tidbits to knit.

# Clog Sox

*Colorful and warm, these SuperQuickKnit socks will warm the feet and hearts of young and old alike. You'll soon master turning a heel and the Kitchener stitch. The trick is to go slow and follow the instructions—and you will have turned the heel before you know it. Debunk the sock mystery, once and for all!*

### SIZES

Child (adult)
*Finished length, heel to toe: 6 (9)" / 15 (23) cm*

### YARN ETC

*Bulky weight yarn: Approx 35 (110) yd / 32 (100 ) m in MC*
*Approx 25 (60) yd / 23 (55) m in CC*
*Double-pointed needles (dpns): Size 8 US (5 mm), size 6 UK, or size needed to obtain gauge*
*Samples in photograph knit in Brown Sheep Bulky, #120 Limeade, #M11 Frost, #M05 Onyx*

### GAUGE

18 sts and 24 rows = 4" / 10 cm in St st

*Always check gauge to save time and ensure correct yardage and correct fit!*

## Sock Top

With MC, cast on 32 (40) sts and distribute on three needles as foll: 12 - 10 - 10 (12 - 14 - 14). Join, being careful not to twist sts. Work in k1, p1 rib for six rnds. Work in St st and stripe pat as follows: **Child**—[three rnds MC, three rnds CC] twice; **adult**—[three rnds CC, three rnds MC] three times, then work three rnds CC.
**Both sizes:** Cut CC yarn.

## Heel Flap

Rearrange sts on three needles as foll: 16 - 8 - 8 (20 - 10 - 10). With MC, work back and forth on the 16 (20) sts for heel flap as foll: **Next row (RS):** *k1, sl 1; rep from *, end k2.
**Next row:** p. Repeat these two rows until heel flap measures 1 (2)" / 2.5 (5) cm, ending with a RS row.

## Turning Heel

**Row 1 (WS):** p10 (12), p2tog, p1, turn work
**Row 2:** sl 1, k5, k2tog, k1, turn
**Row 3:** sl 1, p6, p2tog, p1, turn
**Row 4:** sl 1, k7, k2tog, k1, turn
**Row 5:** sl 1, p8, p2tog, p0 (1), turn

*Child only*

**Row 6:** sl 1, k8, k2tog—10 sts rem

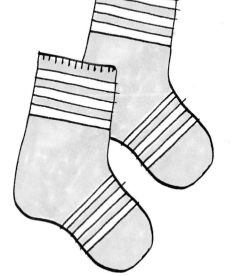

**Row 6:** sl 1, k9, k2tog, k1, turn
**Row 7:** sl 1, p10, p2tog, turn
**Row 8:** sl 1, k10, k2tog—12 sts rem

## GUSSET

With RS of heel flap facing, MC and same needle, pick up and k8 (10) sts along left side of heel flap (needle 1), k next 16 (20) sts for instep (needle 2), pick up and k8 (10) sts along right side of heel flap and k5 (6) sts from heel (needle 3), k rem 5 (6) sts from heel onto needle 1— 13 - 16 - 13 (16 - 20 - 16) sts. **Work dec rnd as foll:** needle 1— k to last three sts, k2tog, k1; needle 2—k; needle 3—k1, k2tog, k rem sts. Rep dec rnd every other rnd a total of 5 (6) times—8 - 16 - 8 (10 - 20 - 10) sts.

## FOOT

K three rnds MC [three rnds CC, three rnds MC] once (twice), and three rnds CC. Cut CC. **Next rnd, dec rnd:** with MC, work as foll: Needle 1—k to last three sts, k2tog, k1; needle 2—k1, k2tog, k to last three sts, k2tog, k1; needle 3—k1, k2tog, k rem sts. K three (four) rnds. Rep dec rnd. K two (three) rnds. Rep dec rnd. K one (two) rnds. Rep dec rnd. K one rnd. Rep dec rnd. K zero (one) rnd. Rep dec

rnd 0 (two) times—6 sts on needle 2, 3 sts on needles 1
and 3. Sl sts from needles 1 and 3 to a single needle—6 sts
rem each needle.

## Finishing: Kitchener Stitch

Weave the last sts tog using Kitchener st, as follows:

1. Bring the yarn needle through the front st as if to p,
   leaving the st on the needle.
2. Bring the yarn needle through the back st as if to k,
   leaving the st on the needle. Bring the yarn needle
   through the same front st as if to k, and then slip this
   st off the needle.
3. Bring the yarn needle through the next front st as
   if to p, again leaving the st on the needle. Bring the
   yarn needle through the first back st as if to p, slip
   the st off.
4. Rep steps 2 and 3 until all sts are used up.

# Oh Baby!

*Adorn the baby in your life with this all-knit classic pullover. You will learn sweater-knitting basics, as well as reverse stockinette neck edging to make that pretty rolled neckline. Simple garter stitch takes more wool than stockinette stitch, but is the easiest stitch to knit and works up into an even, warm fabric.*

## SIZES

Child: 2 (4 - 6) years
*Finished chest:* 25 (28 - 30)" / 63.5 (71 - 76) cm
*Finished length:* 13 (16 - 17½)" / 33 (41 - 44.5) cm

## YARN ETC

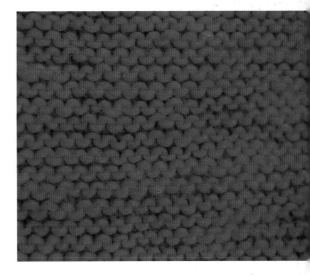

*Aran weight yarn:* Approx 370 (510 - 600) yd / 340 (470 - 550) m
*Needles:* Size 9 US (5.5 mm), size 5 UK, or size needed to obtain gauge
*Circular needle:* 16" (40 cm) length, size 8 US, (5 mm), size 6 UK
*Double-pointed needles (dpns):* Size 9 US (5.5 mm), size 5 UK
Stitch holders
*Sample in photograph knit in Manos del Uruguay, Poppy Red #66*

## GAUGE

16 sts and 28 rows = 4" / 10 cm in garter st

*Always check gauge to save time and ensure correct yardage and correct fit!*

## BACK

Cast on 50 (56 - 60) sts. Work in garter st for 13 (16 - 17½)″ / 33 (41 - 44.5) cm. K15 (17 - 19) sts and place on a holder for shoulder; k20 (22 - 22) sts for neck and place on holder for neck; k rem sts and place on holder for shoulder.

## FRONT

Work same as back until piece measures 11 (13½ - 15)″ / 28 (34.5 - 38) cm from beg.

**Shape neck, next row (RS):** Work 20 (22 - 24) sts, join second ball of yarn and k center 10 (12 - 12) sts and place on holder, work to end. Working both sides at once, bind off from each neck edge 2 sts once, dec 1 st every other row three times—15 (17 - 19) sts rem. Work even until same length as back. Place rem sts on holders for shoulders.

## SHOULDER SEAMS

With *wrong sides* facing each other and front of sweater facing you, place sts of back and front right shoulder on

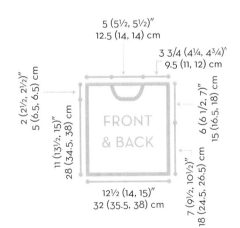

5 (5½, 5½)″
12.5 (14, 14) cm

3 3/4 (4¼, 4¾)″
9.5 (11, 12) cm

2 (2½, 2½)″
5 (6.5, 6.5) cm

FRONT
& BACK

11 (13½, 15)″
28 (34.5, 38) cm

6 (6 1/2, 7)″
15 (16.5, 18) cm

7 (9½, 10½)″
18 (24.5, 26.5) cm

12½ (14, 15)″
32 (35.5, 38) cm

two parallel dpns. With a third dpn, k first st from front needle tog with first st from back needle, *k next st from front and back needles tog, sl first st over second st to bind off; rep from * until all sts are bound off. Work in same way for left shoulder.

## SLEEVES

Mark for sleeves 6 (6½ - 7)" / 15 (16.5 - 18) cm down from shoulder seam on front and back. With RS facing, pick up and k48 (52 - 56) sts between markers. Work in garter st, working 3 (7 - 7) rows even, then dec 1 st each edge on next row, then every fourth (sixth - sixth) row 9 (10 - 12) times more—28 (30 - 30) sts rem. Work even until sleeve measures 6 (11 - 12½)" / 15 (28 - 32) cm. Bind off.

## FINISHING

Sew side and sleeve seams. **Neckband:** With RS facing and circular needle (or dpns), start at right shoulder and pick up 14 (16 - 16) sts along right neck edge, k sts from front holder, pick up 14 (16 - 16) sts along left neck edge, k sts from back holder—k58 (66 - 66) sts. K four rnds. Bind off.

12 (13, 14)"
30 (33, 35.5) cm

SLEEVE

6 (11, 12½)"
15 (28, 32) cm

7 (7½, 7½)"
18 (19, 19) cm

# Pop Top

*Mimic Swedish teens and sport this jaunty cap, perfect for outdoor sports or city streets. The hat shown is done in cotton, for three-season wear, but it would be fabulous in warm wool as well. This pattern will introduce you to five-needle knitting. You'll also learn how to make a zany tassel topknot!*

## SIZES

Baby (toddler - child - adult)
*Finished hat size:* 16 (18 - 20 - 22)" / 41 (46 - 51 - 56) cm

## YARN ETC

*DK weight yarn:* Approx 40 (45 - 55 -70) yd / 37 (41 - 50 - 65) cm each in colors A and B
*DK weight yarn:* Small amounts in colors C and D
*One set (five) double-pointed needles (dpns):* Size 5 US (3.75 mm), size 9 UK, or size needed to obtain gauge
*Circular needle:* 16" (40 cm) length, size 5 US (3.75 mm), size 9 UK or smaller
Tapestry needle
*Sample in photograph knit in Berroco's Cotton Twist Linoleum #8372 (A), Sea Glass #8368 (B), True Red #8311 (C), and Sea Goddess Blue #8335 (D)*

## GAUGE

22 sts and 30 rows = 4" / 10 cm in St st

 *Always check gauge to save time and ensure correct yardage and correct fit!*

## Hat

Beg at top with A and dpns, cast on 4 sts to one needle. Inc 1 st in each st and divide these 8 sts evenly over four needles. Join, taking care not to twist sts on needle. Work in St st (k every rnd), inc 1 st in last st on each needle every rnd (therefore inc 4 sts every rnd) until there are 88 (100 - 112 - 124) sts. Cut A, join B, and work even in St st for 2 (2 - 2½ - 3½)" / 5 (5 - 6.5 - 9) cm from last inc rnd, or desired depth. Transfer sts to circular needle.

## I-Cord Edging

With two dpns and MC, cast on 4 sts. K3, then, with RS of hat facing, k last st tog with first st from circular needle. * Do not turn work. Slide sts to other end of needle to work next row from RS and k3, k last st tog with next st from circular needle; rep from * until all sts from hat are worked. Bind off and sew ends of I-cord tog.

## Pop Top Tassel

Cut a 3½ yd / 3.5 m length of A. Using tapestry needle, sew through top of hat, making forty 3" / 7.5 cm loops.

With B, start at top of hat and tightly wrap loops for 2½" / 6.5 cm up from crown. Weave in ends. Cut loops to make tassel top.

## TRIM

With C, make 50" / 127 cm chain; don't cut yarn. Sew around hat in curlicues as seen in photograph, adjusting length as necessary. Cut yarn and pull end through loop.

## DUPLICATE STITCH

With D, work a duplicate stitch here and there on either side of the chain trim. A duplicate stitch covers a knit stitch with a contrasting color yarn of the same weight. Bring the needle up below the stitch to be worked. Insert the needle under both loops one row above, and pull it through. Insert the needle back into the stitch below, and through the center of the next stitch.

# Doggie Mac

*Reward the canine fashion plates in your family with a warm, waterproof coat, fit for all weathers! This is a perfect opportunity to practice your plaiding and felting skills or to try out these techniques for the first time.*

## SIZES

Extra-small (small) dog
*Finished chest (after felting):* Approx 15 (18)" / 38 (46) cm
*Finished length (after felting):* Approx 13 (17)" / 33 (43) cm

## YARN ETC

*Bulky weight wool:* Approx 170 (270) yd / 155 (245) m in MC
Approx 10 (20) yd / 9 (18) m in CC
*Needles:* Size 11 US (8 mm), size 0 UK, or size needed to obtain gauge
Two buttons
Yarn needle
*Sample in photograph knit in Brown Sheep Bulky, Limeaid #M120 and Clematis #M56*

## GAUGE

Before felting: 12 sts and 16 rows = 4" / 10 cm in St st
After felting: 14 sts and 20 rows = 4" / 10 cm

*Always check gauge to save time and ensure correct yardage and correct fit!*

## Sweater

Beg at lower back edge, with MC cast on 29 (35) sts. K four rows. **Next row (RS):** k3, inc in next st, k to last 4 sts, inc in next st, k3. **Next row:** k3, inc in next st, p to last 4 sts, inc in next st, k3. Rep last two rows until there are 41 (49) sts. Work even, keeping first and last 3 sts in garter st and rem sts in St st for 14 (18) rows. **Straps:** Cast on 8 (9) sts at beg of next two rows—57 (67) sts. Work first and last 3 sts in garter st and rem sts in St st for four rows. Bind off 8 (9) sts at beg of next two rows—41 (49) sts. Cont to work first and last 3 sts in garter st and rem sts in St st, and, *at the same time,* inc 1 st each side every sixth (eighth) row 3 (4) times as follows: **On RS row:** k3, inc, work to last 4 sts, inc in next st, k3—47 (57) sts. Work even until 24 (36) rows have been worked from last bind off row. **Shape neck, next row (RS):** Keeping first and last 3 sts in garter st, work 17 (20) sts, join second ball of yarn and bind off center 13 (17) sts, work rem sts. Working both sides with separate balls of yarn, p next row.

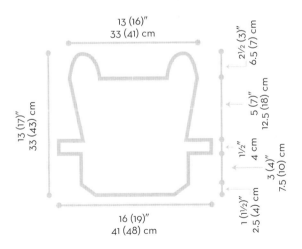

13 (16)"
33 (41) cm

16 (19)"
41 (48) cm

13 (17)"
33 (43) cm

2½ (3)"
6.5 (7) cm

5 (7)"
12.5 (18) cm

1½"
4 cm

3 (4)"
7.5 (10) cm

1 (1½)"
2.5 (4) cm

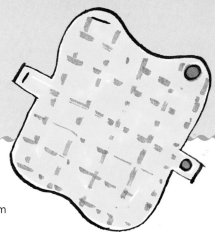

**Next row (RS):** *k3, k2tog, k to last 5 sts, k2tog, k3; with other ball, rep from *. Rep last two rows until 7 (8) sts rem each side. Bind off.

## Weaving Plaid

Fold sweater in half lengthwise and mark center line of sts. With RS facing and yarn needle, weave a strand of CC in and out along this line. Cont to weave vertical stripes of CC on either side of center every seventh st. Starting on eighth row from bottom border, weave horizontal stripes every eighth row.

## Felting

Due to temperature fluctuations, felting time will vary. Check often for sizing. In washing machine, set on hot wash/cold rinse for a small load, place sweater in water with 1 tsp of dishwashing liquid detergent, and run through longest cycle. Check size, then run through again if necessary. Remove, lay sweater flat, and let dry.

## Finishing

With sharp scissors, carefully cut a small buttonhole in one strap and sew button to other strap. Cut another buttonhole 3 sts in from left neck edge. Sew button to other side.

## Notes

The size of the garment is made larger to account for shrinkage after piece is felted. The finished size of a felted garment can be affected by the type of yarn you are using as well as the temperature of water in your washing machine. The measurements here are consequently approximate, and it may take some experimentation to achieve the desired size.

Different wools and colors may felt more or less, making a smaller or larger garment and thus may require different amounts of yarn to achieve the desired size. For best results, use a single-ply, roving type yarn.

# Tree Topper

Delight city shoppers and holiday merrymakers with this head-turner of a hat! The tree hat is perfect for all the little ones in your life. Embellish it any way you please, with buttons, bobbles, bells, or bows. The I-cord trim twists around the simple conical shape. For perfect shaping, keep careful track of your rows and decreases.

## SIZES

Baby (toddler)
*Finished hat size:* 16 (18)" / 41 (46) cm

## YARN ETC

*Bulky weight yarn:* Approx 100 (110) yd / 92 (100) m in MC (green)
Approx 25 (30) yd / 23 (28) m in color A (red)
Approx 30 (35) yd / 28 (32) m in color B (white)
*Needles:* Size 8 US (5 mm), size 6 UK, or size needed to obtain gauge
*Double-pointed needles (dpns):* Size 8 US (5 mm), size 6 UK
Ten small decorative buttons
*Sample in photograph knit in Reynolds Lopi, #212 green, #78 red, #51 white*
*Buttons from www.zecca.net*

## GAUGE

18 sts and 24 rows = 4" / 10 cm in St st

*Always check gauge to save time and ensure correct yardage and correct fit!*

## HAT

With A and straight
needles, cast on 71 (80) sts.
Starting with a p row, work
in St st for ten rows, inc
10 sts evenly across last
row—81 (90) sts. Change to
MC and cont in St st until
piece measures 6" / 15 cm from cast-on edge, ending with
a p row. **Next row, dec row 1 (RS):** *k7, k2tog; rep from
*—72 (80) sts. Cont in St st and work a dec row every
sixth row as foll:

**Dec row 2 (RS):** *k6, k2tog; rep from *—63 (70) sts
**Dec row 3 (RS):** *k5, k2tog; rep from *—54 (60) sts
**Dec row 4 (RS):** *k4, k2tog; rep from *—45 (50) sts
**Dec row 5 (RS):** *k3, k2tog; rep from *—36 (40) sts
**Dec row 6 (RS):** *k2, k2tog; rep from *—27 (30) sts
**Dec row 7 (RS):** *k1, k2tog; rep from *—18 (20) sts
**Dec row 8 (RS):** *k2tog; rep from *—9 (10) sts
**Dec row 9 (RS):** *k2tog; rep from *, end k1 (0)—5 sts
Cut yarn, leaving a long end for sewing and draw through
rem sts on needle.

## FINISHING

Sew back seam, sewing first ten rows on opposite side for roll. With B, make a 2" / 5 cm pompom as foll: Wind yarn 30 times around index and middle finger. Cut a 12" / 30 cm length, and tie around middle. Cut ends, and trim to 2" / 5 cm as evenly as possible. Using the 12" / 30 cm length, sew to top of hat.

## I-Cord Trim

With dpns and B, cast on 4 sts. **Next row (RS):** k3. Do not turn. Slide sts to beg of needle to work next row from RS. Rep from * until I-cord measures approx 60" / 152 cm. Do not cut yarn; place sts on a small holder or safety pin. Beg at top of hat, baste cord around hat to just above red brim (see photo for placement), adjusting length of cord if necessary. Cut yarn, pull end through 4 sts, and secure. Sew cord in place. Sew on buttons as desired.

# SNOW
## *Snow*
## SNOW

*Cold weather charmers . . .*

*in a wintry mix of dash and style*

WHEN IT SNOWS WE ALL want to knit up hats and mitts and neckwarmers, too. The mittens here become extra-warm as the roving is knit inside, a soft downy filling for cold fingers. All SuperQuickKnits, these projects are just the place to use your specialty yarns with bobbles and flair.

# Stuffie Mitts

*Light up the skating pond with these SuperQuickKnit mittens, great for kids or adults. They're easy to make on two needles, with roving knit in. The bird's eye pattern makes for automatic insulation as the roving is fulled inside the mitten.*

## SIZES

Child (adult)

## YARN ETC

*Bulky weight yarn:* Approx 100 (110) yd / 92 (100) m in MC
*½" / 1.25 cm thick natural roving:* 1 oz / 28 gm
*Needles:* Size 10 US (6 mm), size 4 UK, or size needed to obtain gauge
Stitch holders
Stitch markers
*Sample in photograph knit in JCA / Reynolds Lopi #868*

## GAUGE

14 sts and 20 rows = 4" / 10 cm in pat

 *Always check gauge to save time and ensure correct yardage and correct fit!*

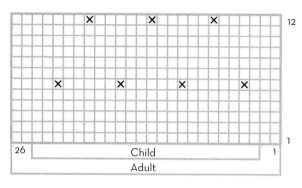

12

26    Child

1

Adult

1

Color Key

**X** Roving

## KNITTING IN ROVING

Pull roving apart into approx 4" / 10 cm long pieces. Follow chart, knitting in roving as follows: Insert needle into st, lay piece of roving over inserted needle, holding ends to the back, then wrap MC yarn as usual, knitting both roving and yarn into the same st. On next row (WS), insert needle into both roving and MC yarn to purl. When knitting is done, you may need to adjust roving sts so that MC yarn does not show.

## RIGHT MITT

Cast on 22 (26) sts. Work in St st and chart pat for 2 (3)" / 5 (7.5) cm, ending with a RS row. **Next row (WS):** Work 13 (14) sts, place M, p3, place M, work 6 (9) sts.

## THUMB GORE

**Next row (RS), inc row:** Keeping to pat, inc in st after first M and before second M. Cont to work in pats as established, working inc row every RS row until there are 9 (9) sts between markers, ending with a RS row. **Next row (WS):** Work to M and place sts on a holder, work 9 (9) sts and leave on needle, work rem sts and place on a holder.

## Thumb

Join yarn and cont on thumb sts only as foll: cast on 0 (1) st at beginning of next two rows—9 (11) sts. Work even in St st and pat for 6 (8) more rows. **Next row (RS):** k1, *k2tog; rep from * across row. Cut yarn, leaving a long end and pull through rem sts. Sew thumb seam.

## Hand

Place sts from first holder onto needle and work sts in pat, pick up and k3 sts across thumb gusset, work sts from second holder—22 (26) sts. Cont in St st and pat until hand measures 3 (4)" / 7.5 (10) cm above thumb, ending with a WS row.

## Top Shaping

**Row 1 (RS):** k4 (3) , k2tog, [k2 (4), k2 tog] three times, k4 (3)—18 (22) sts rem

**Rows 2 and 4:** p

**Row 3:** k3 (2) , k2tog, [k1 (3), k2tog] three times, k4 (3)—14 (18) sts rem

**Row 5:** k2tog across—7 (9) sts rem

Cut yarn, pull through rem sts, and sew back seam. Weave in all loose ends.

### Left Mitt

Cast on 22 (26) sts and work as for right mitt for 2 (3)" / 5 (7.5) cm, ending with a RS row. **Next row (WS):** p6 (9) sts, place M, p3, place M, p 13 (14) sts. Work thumb gore and complete as for right mitt.

# Ski Chamonix

*The ski slopes will reverberate with this colorful double-knit delight. If you know both Continental and English knitting, use both at the same time, one color for each, to speed up this QuickKnit hat.*

## SIZES

Baby (toddler, child, adult)
*Finished hat size:* 14 (16 - 18 - 22)" / 35.5 (41 - 46 - 56) cm

## YARN ETC

*Worsted weight yarn:* Approx 95 (105 - 115 - 125) yd / 87 (96 - 105 - 115) m in MC
Approx 20 yd / 19 m in each of colors A, B, C, and D
*Needles:* Sizes 7 and 8 US (4.5 mm and 5 mm), sizes 7 and 6 UK, or sizes needed to achieve gauge
*Sample in photograph knit in Brown Sheep's Lamb's Pride, Red Baron #81 (MC), Aztec Turquoise #78 (A), Lotus Pink #38 (B), Limeaid #120 (C), Orange You Glad #110 (D)*

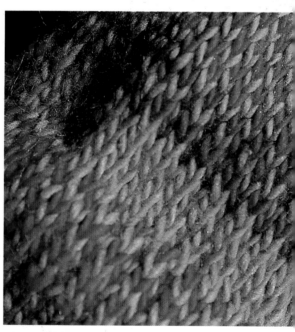

## GAUGE

19 sts and 20 rows = 4" / 10 cm in fair isle pat

*Always check gauge to save time and ensure correct yardage and correct fit!*

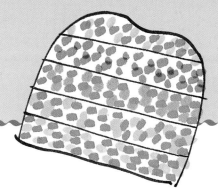

## HAT

With smaller needles and MC, cast on 67 (77 - 87 - 105).
Starting with a p row, work in St st for eleven rows. **Next
row (RS):** p, for turning ridge. Change to larger needles
and work in St st following chart until piece measures
4 (5 - 6 - 7)" / 10 (12.5 - 15 - 18) cm from turning ridge,
ending with a WS row. **Next row, dec row:** Keeping to pat,
k2tog across, end k1. Cont to k2tog across all RS rows until
5 (5 - 6 - 7) sts rem. Cut yarn, leaving long end. Pull
through rem sts and sew back seam. Fold hem under at
turning ridge and stitch in place.

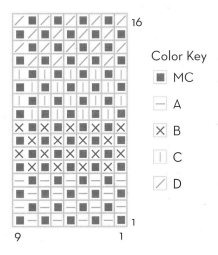

Color Key

■ MC

— A

✕ B

❘ C

╱ D

# Snow Bandeau

*Sparkling with tiny bobbles, this smart bandeau ties in a back bow adorned with refined pompoms, an elegant touch for a crisp evening. Three strands of yarn are used held together for this project, resulting in a rich, sumptuous mix. Try to find a specialty yarn that will give a spark to your mohair.*

## SIZES

Child (adult)
*Finished measurement:* 3" × 16" (4" × 21") / 7.5 cm × 41 cm (10 cm × 52 cm)

## YARN ETC

Use a combination of three faux fur and novelty yarns that when knit tog will knit to gauge shown below.
*Faux fur and novelty yarns:* Approx 50 (70) yd / 45 (65) m each in colors A, B, and C
*Needles:* Size 13 US (9 mm), size 00 UK, or size needed to obtain gauge
*Crochet hook:* Size G US (4 mm), size 8 UK
*Sample in photograph knit in Berroco's Furz #3034 (A), Furz #3806 (B), and Bubble Effects #8423 (C)*

## GAUGE

11 sts = 4" / 10 cm in St st using three strands held tog

 *Always check gauge to save time and ensure correct yardage and fit!*

## BANDEAU

With one strand of each color A, B, and C held tog, cast on 44 (54) sts. Work in St st for 1½ (2)" / 4 (5) cm, ending with a k row. **Next row (WS):** k for turning ridge. Cont in St st starting with k row until piece measures 3 (4)" / 7.5 (10) cm from turning ridge, ending with a k row. **Next row (WS):** k for turning ridge. Cont in St st starting with k row until piece measures 1½ (2)" / 4 (5) cm from second turning ridge, ending with a p row. Bind off loosely knitwise.

## FINISHING

Fold top and bottom edges under at turning ridges and sew cast on and bound off edges together so that seam will be at center back of band. Sew side edges closed. With crochet hook and colors A and B held tog, make two 11" / 28 cm chains. Sew one to each end of band. Make two 1" / 2.5 cm pompoms and sew to end of each chain. Wind yarn 30 times around index and middle finger. Cut a 12" / 30 cm length, and tie around middle. Cut ends, and trim to 1" / 2.5 cm as evenly as possible. Using the 12" / 30 cm length, sew to ends of chain.

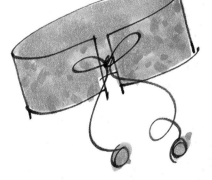

# Elf Cap

*The tassels and ties make this SuperQuickKnit a winner. Why knit it? Why ever not? It's the simplest, cutest two-hour cap on the planet. It's also a wonderful way to learn seed stitch, where you knit the purls and purl the knits, making a fabric that lays flat and holds detail.*

## SIZES

Baby (toddler, child, adult)
*Finished size:* 15 (16 - 19 - 21)" / 37.5 (41 - 48 - 53.5) cm

## YARN ETC

*Super-bulky yarn:* Approx 60 (70 - 80 - 90) yd / 55 (65 - 75 - 85) m
*Needles:* Size 13 US (9 mm), size 00 UK, or size needed to obtain gauge
Cable needle (CN)
*Crochet hook:* Size H US (5 mm), size 6 UK
Two stitch markers
*Sample in photograph knit in Rowan's Big Wool #006*

## GAUGE

10 sts and 18 rows = 4" / 10 cm in seed st

*Always check gauge to save time and ensure correct yardage and correct fit!*

## Note

Requiring just two needles, seed stitch is a very useful pattern to have in your repertoire. When working in seed stitch, take care to bring the yarn to the front or back before you remove the stitch from the needle. This speeds the process up, and makes achieving an even tension easier.

## Seed Stitch Pattern

All rows: k1, *p1, k1; rep from * for seed stitch pattern

## Cable Knit Pattern

Row 1 and all WS rows: p6
Rows 2, 6, 8, and 10: k6
Rows 4 and 12: sl 3 sts to cable needle, hold in back, k3; k3 sts from cable needle
Repeat rows 5 to 12 for cable pattern

## CAP

Cast on 36 (40 - 48 - 52) sts. **Row 1 (WS):** Work 15 (17 - 21 - 23) sts in seed st; put marker (M) on needle, work 6 sts in cable; put M on needle, work 15 (17 - 21 - 23) sts in seed st. Work in pats as established until piece measures 3½ (4 - 4 - 4½)" / 9 (10 - 10 - 11.5) cm, ending with a WS row. Keeping to pat, dec 1 st each edge next row and all RS rows 13 (15 - 7 - 9) times—10 (10 - 34 - 34) sts rem. **Child and adult only:** Cont to work decs on RS rows until 10 sts rem as follows: k2tog, work to 2 sts before first M, k2tog, work to next M, k2tog after M, work to last 2 sts, k2tog. **All sizes, next RS row:** k2tog across— 5 sts rem. Cut yarn, leaving long end and pull through rem sts. Sew back seam, stopping 4 (5 - 5 - 5½)" / 10 (12.5 - 12.5 - 14) cm from bottom edge.

## TASSEL

Wind yarn around four fingers 30 times. Cut yarn. Cut 12" / 30 cm piece, pull through center, and tie tight knot. Cut another piece and tie around all ends, 1" / 2.5 cm down from top. Cut bottom loops and trim evenly to 3" / 7.5 cm. Sew firmly to top of cap.

## TIES

With crochet hook, make two 12" / 30 cm chains. Sew one securely to each ear flap.

# Noel Noel

Charm St. Nick with this monogrammed holiday stocking, all decked out with crochet and bobble trim. You will learn to knit a basic sock, change colors, knit duplicate stitch monograms, and make simple bobbles.

## SIZE

Finished length: 19" / 48 cm

## YARN ETC

Bulky weight yarn, as below. Two balls of red and one ball each of other colors will make both stockings.

*Stripes (at right in photo on facing page):*
60 yd / 55 m in color A (red)
40 yd / 37 m in color B (green)
85 yd / 80 m in color C (perwinkle)
5 yd / 5 m in color D (celery)

*Jester (at left in photo on facing page):*
25 yd / 23 m in color A (gold)
90 yd / 85 m in color B (red)
12 yd / 11 m in color C (periwinkle)
40 yd / 37 m in color D (green)
5 yd / 5 m in color E (celery)

*Needles:* Size 10 US (6mm), size 4 UK, or size needed to achieve gauge
*Double pointed needles (dpns):* Size 10 US (6mm), size 4 UK
Stitch markers
*Crochet hook:* Size I US (5.5 mm), size 5 UK
*Samples in photograph knit in Reynolds / JCA Lopi. Stripes (right): Red #78, Green #212, Periwinkle #390, and Celery #369; Jester (left): Gold #72, Red #78, Periwinkle #390, Green #212, and Celery #369*

Always check gauge to save time and ensure correct yardage and fit!

## GAUGE

14 sts and 20 rows = 4" / 10 cm in St st

## Stocking Tops

*Stripes (at right in photo on facing page)*

With A and straight needles, cast on 45 sts. Work four rows in seed st. With B and starting with a p row, work twelve rows St st. With B, p two rows, k one row. In St st starting with a k row, work stripe pat as foll: [nine rows in C, four rows in B] twice, nine rows in C.

*Jester (at left in photo on facing page)*

Points (make 5): With A and straight needles, cast on 1 st. **Row 1:** k into front and back of st (inc). **Row 2:** k2. **Row 3:** Inc, k1. **Rows 4 and 5:** k3. Inc 1 st beg and end of next row, then every third row twice more—9 sts. **Next row:** k9. Sl sts to spare needle. Work four more points, adding them to same spare needle—45 sts on needle. **Join points:** With A, k two rows. With B, k four rows. Starting with a k row, work twelve rows in St st. With A, k two rows, p one row. With B, starting with a p row, work seven rows St st. **Pat row 1 (RS):** k4 B, *k1 C, k5 B; rep from *, end k4 B. With B, work five rows St st. **Pat row 2 (RS):** k1 B, *k1 D, k5 B; rep from *, end k2 B. With B, work five rows St st. Rep Pat row 1. With B, work four rows St st.

**The following instructions are written for Stripes with changes for Jester in ( ).**

## Seed Stitch

Row 1: *k, p1; rep from *, end k1.

Row 2 and all other rnds: p the k sts and k the p sts.

## Bobbles

With dpn, cast on 2 sts. Sl sts to right end of needle. K1, k into front and back of next st. Turn, p 3. Turn, k1, k2tog. Turn, k2tog. Pull end through loop. Fold in half and sew to hat.

## Soutache

With crochet hook, work crochet chain for about 40″ / 102 cm, leaving yarn attached. With yarn needle, sew in swirls around stocking, meeting at back seam.

## HEEL FLAP

Sl first 11 sts to dpn 1. Place next 23 sts on another dpn. Sl rem 11 sts to dpn 1. Work back and forth on these 22 sts for the heel flap as foll: With color A (D), *k1, sl 1; repeat from * across. **Next row:** p. Repeat these two rows until heel flap measures 2" / 5 cm, ending with a RS row. **Turn heel, next row:** p13, p2tog, p1. Turn, sl 1, k5, k2tog, k1. Turn, sl 1, p6, p2tog, p1. Turn, sl 1, k7, k2tog, k1. Turn, sl 1, p8, p2tog, p1. Turn, sl 1, k9, k2tog, k1. Turn, sl 1, p10, p2tog, p1. Turn, sl 1, k11, k2tog, k1—14 sts rem.

## GUSSET

With same dpn (needle 1) and C (B), pick up and k9 sts along left side of heel flap. With another dpn (needle 2), k 11, k2tog, k10 sts for instep. With another dpn (needle 3), pick up and k9 sts along right side of heel flap, k7 sts from needle 1—16 - 22 - 16 sts on needles 1, 2, and 3 respectively. **Next rnd:** k. **Next rnd:** With needle 1, k to last 3 sts, k2tog, k1; with needle 2, k. With needle 3, k1, k2tog, k rem sts. Rep last two rnds a total of five times—11 - 22 - 11 sts rem.

## STOCKING FOOT AND TOE

*Stripes:* k four rnds C, four rnds B, nine rnds C. *Jester:* k two rnds B, one rnd C, four rnds B, one rnd D, four rnds B, one rnd C, four rnds B. **Toe:** With A (D) work dec rnd: With needle 1, work to last 3 sts, k2tog, k1; with needle 2, k1, k2tog, k to last 3 sts, k2tog, k1. With needle 3, k1, k2tog,

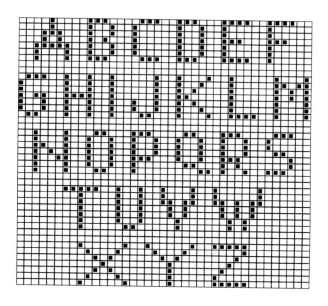

k rem sts. K four rnds even. Work dec rnd. K three rnds even. Work dec rnd. K two rnds even. [Work dec rnd. K one rnd even] twice. Work three more dec rnds—3 - 6 - 3 sts rem. Place first 3 sts from needle 2 back on needle 1, and the last 3 sts on needle 2 back on needle 3—6 sts on each needle. Weave the last sts tog.

## FINISHING

Sew back seam. **Hanging loop:** With A (B), single-crochet twelve loops. Form loop and sew to back seam.

*Stripes:* Work soutache and bobbles, and attach as in the photograph. Following chart, duplicate st name or initials across top band. Duplicate st covers a knit stitch with a contrasting color yarn of the same weight. Bring the needle up below the st to be worked. Insert the needle under both loops one row above, and pull it through. Insert the needle back into the st below, and through the center of the next st.

*Jester:* Work soutache and attach to create name. *Optional:* With double strand of B, duplicate st over first row of color B below points. This will hide color change and make points stand up straighter.

# Hats Off!

At the end of months of working on a book of this size I am ever grateful to my merry band of enormously talented co-workers. So here is resounding thanks to Nina Fuller, who takes all the extraordinary photos . . . to Carla Scott, the technical wizard who writes the patterns . . . to Judith Shangold, fabulously deft pattern writer, proofreader, and editor . . . and to Isabel Smiles for her clear design eye.

## ABOUT JIL AND HER TEAM

### JIL EATON

Trained as a painter and graphic designer at Skidmore College, Colby College, and the Graduate School of Design at Harvard University, Jil Eaton's working life as an artist, graphic designer, arts administrator, and restauranteur led her in many disparate directions. She never dreamed she would take her love of knitting to a professional level. But after the birth of her son, Alexander, Jil began creating one-of-a-kind outfits for him, which led to the birth of her company, MinnowKnits.

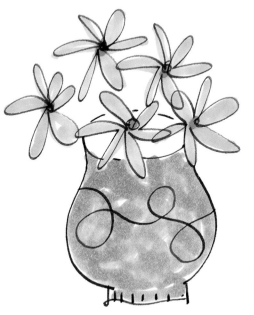

Jil now designs, publishes, and distributes internationally an independent line of hand-knitting patterns for children's wear under the acclaimed MinnowKnits™ label, as well as authoring knitting books. Her designs have a comfortable but chic silhouette, encompassing both the traditional and outré, adapting everything in easy-to-knit projects with astute attention to detail, fresh styling, and off-beat colorways. Smitten with color, and with an eye toward fashion, Jil's inspiration comes from everywhere, including the glossy pages of *Vogue*, the streets of Paris and New York, and paintings in museums. Jil produces two pattern collections annually, designs for *Vogue Knitting International* and other publications, and is busy with her sixth book. Always returning to her deep-seeded love of knitting, designing knitwear focuses all her talents. Jil lives in Portland, Maine, with her husband David, her son Alexander, and her enormous dog Zachary, who even gets a sweater once in a while!

## NINA FULLER

Nina Fuller is the one who so wonderfully captures all these charming models on film. A nationally acclaimed location and studio photographer, Nina has degrees in

photography, painting, and printmaking
from Silvermine College of Art and
George Washington University. Always
on her toes, always with a camera in
hand, Nina has a gift for catching the
right angle, finding the most beautiful
light, capturing the exact moment when
the tear falls or the smile breaks.
Location photography has emerged as

a creative focus for Nina, and her major clients include
LL Bean, Land's End, Atlantic Records, and—last but not
least—MinnowKnits International. Her on-the-spot location
work with people is rarely matched, as her inimitable
charm and energy transfix her beguiled subjects.

Nina lives in Maine with her two beautiful children
Spencer and Lily, who we often see through her camera
lens in MinnowKnits books and patterns. Growing up in
the studio, constantly in front of one camera or another,
both have a presence and inner light, as does Nina.

## CARLA SCOTT

Carla Scott is my pattern writer, technical editor, and
general knitting wizard. Working as a knitting professional
throughout her career, Carla is without peer in her

fabulous knowledge of knitting and garment structure. Since the beginning, she has translated my design concepts into written instructions and comprehensive charts. She lights up when presented with a new design challenge, figuring out details that would give me a headache. She is clear and calm amidst a mountain of math and engineering. Carla is now Executive Editor at *Vogue Knitting* and, as always, is delightful to work with.

## JUDITH SHANGOLD

Judith Shangold and her assistant Janice Bye are crucial to the technical success of my work. Judith takes on the tricky and enormous task of reviewing all the patterns and charts at many different stages for accuracy, consistency, and clarity; she also has been the technical pattern writer for several patterns for this book. A designer herself, Judith publishes her own work under Designs by Judith and A Bear in Sheep's Clothing. She also distributes MinnowKnits patterns and Manos del Uruguay yarns through her company, Design Source.

## THE KNITTERS

I am blessed to have hand knitters with an eye for perfection and professional craftsmanship. A book such as

this requires knitting prototypes, which without doubt seem to result in knitting emergencies, last minute changes and re-knits, and midnight queries. Knitting under the gun is an ordeal, as one can only knit so fast, never mind accurately and to gauge. The results of these knitters is, as ever, extraordinary.

Nita Young was the master knitter on this book, knitting the lion's share of the model garments beautifully and quickly. Lucinda Heller whipped up the huge Weekend Pullover right on schedule. Peggy Lewis, who knits like lightning, made various accessories and Bow Cardi. Shirley LaBranche garter stitched Oh Baby. Joan Cassidy knit Capri Cable and Tippet with her extraordinary, perfect touch.

## Models
Designing a collection fit for beginners has been a challenge, and this group of models, young and grown alike, has given spunk and charm to these chic garments.

Tippet: Petra Dio
Elf Cap: Fionn Desmond & Ellie Desmond
Weekend Pullover: Spencer Hoffman & Petra Dio
Daisy Hat: Gail Henry & Dylan Henry-Tingle

**Bow Cardi:** Sofia McNally

**Capri Cable:** Lovey Marino

**Chic Chapeau & Mitts:** Julliette Holmes-Smith & Mary Elizabeth Badger

**Bohemian Wrap-City:** Ryan Fuller

**Demi Deux:** Alex Carter

**Cashmere Crème:** Ryan Fuller

**Clog Sox:** Destry Sibley, Lily Hoffman, Mariah Monks, & Max Monks

**Oh Baby:** Mia Spencer

**Pop Top:** Mariah Monks

**Doggie Mac:** Loki and Cosmos Monks

**Tree Topper:** Emma Davis

**Snow Bandeau:** Tunde & Emma Schwartz

**Stuffie Mitts:** Kathryn Buxton and Jane Ackerman

**Ski Chamonix:** Destry Sibley, Lily Hoffman, & Spencer Hoffman

**Italiano:** Lovey Marino

Thanks to the Golden Giraffe Children's Shop, 32 Exchange Street, Portland, Maine, for loaning us so many charming children's garments for photo shoots.

## Etc

Other enormous thanks go to my extraordinary and esteemed publisher Anne Knudsen, and to my visionary art director, Kim Bartko. Thanks also to my mother, Nancy Whipple Lord, for teaching me to knit, and to my grandmother, Flora Hall Whipple for teaching *her* to knit. Thanks to Tunde Schwartz, my studio assistant, who calmly helped me keep all the balls in the air, with intelligence, perfection, grace, and constant good humor, and for modeling as well! Thanks, each and every one of you, I couldn't do it without you!

# Shopping Notes

All the gorgeous yarns and products used in this book are available from the following distributors. You can depend on any of these labels for yarns that are of the highest quality, some of the most beautiful yarns on the market. Contact them for shops in your area. Always knit with the very best yarns and materials you can afford . . . remember, you're knitting heirlooms!

## YARNS

**Berroco**
14 Elmdale Road
PO Box 367
Uxbridge, MA 01569-0367
508-278-2527
*www.berroco.com*

**Brown Sheep**
100662 County Road 16
Mitchell, NE 69357
308-635-2198
*www.brownsheep.com*

**Manos Del Uruguay**
Design Source
(US Distributor)
38 Montvale, Suite 145
Stoneham, MA 02180
781-438-9631

**Rowan Yarns**
Westminster Fibers
4 Townsend West, Unit #8
Nashua, NH 03063
603-886-5041
*www.knitrowan.com*

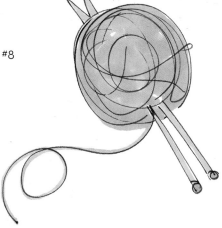

**Reynolds**
c/o JCA
35 Scales Lane
Townsend, MA 01469-1094
978-597-8794
*www.jcacrafts.com*

**Trendsetter Yarns**
16742 Stagg Street
Van Nuys, CA 91406
818-780-5497

## NEEDLES

**Addi Turbos**
Skacel Collection, Inc.
224 SW 12th Street
Renton, WA 98055
213-854-2710

**Crystal Palace**
2320 Bissell Ave.
Richmond, CA 94804
510-237-9988

## BUTTONS

**Zecca (Hand Made Fimo Buttons)**
PO Box 1664
Lakeville, CT 06039
860-435-2211
*www.zecca.net*

**Central Yarn**
53 Oak Street
Portland, ME 04101
207-775-0852
*www.centralyarn.com*

# Must-Have Books

Editors of *Vogue Knitting*, **Vogue Knitting**. New York, Sixth and Spring Books, 2002. One of my favorites, this book is rich in history and great for technique, with clear illustrations for just about everything. I require it for my knitting classes, and it has good basic design information with some traditional patterns. If you just buy one book, buy this.

Hiatt, June Hemons. **The Principles of Knitting**. New York, Simon & Schuster, 1988. This book is unbelievably out of print, but is wonderful if you can find it!

Goldberg, Rhoda Ochser. **The New Knitting Dictionary** New York, Crown Publishers, 1984.

Newton, Deborah. **Designing Knitwear**. Taunton Press, 1992. A fabulous book on design, including history, technique, and new ways to see.

Standfield, Lesley. **The New Knitting Stitch Library**. Chilton Book Company, 1992. Comprehensive, with some new stitches for inspiration as you become more accomplished and branch out with new stitch techniques.

Stanley, Montse. *The Handknitter's Handbook*. London: David and Charles, 1986. Great source for various cast-on techniques.

Square, Vicki. *The Knitter's Companion*. Interweave Press, 1996. Tuck this into your knitting bag for a quick, convenient reference book.

Zimmerman, Elizabeth. *Knitter's Almanac*. Dover Publications (reprint). New York: Dover Publications, 1981.

———. *Knitting Without Tears*. New York: Simon & Schuster (reprint), 1973. Fabulous for beginners!

# Abbreviations & Explanations

| | | | | |
|---|---|---|---|---|
| **approx** | Approximately | | **rem** | Remaining |
| **beg** | Beginning | | **rep** | Repeat(s) |
| **CC** | Contrasting color | | **rev St st** | Reverse stockinette stitch—k all WS rows, p all RS rows |
| **cont** | Continue(ing)s | | **rib** | Rib(bing) |
| **CN** | Cable needle | | **rnd(s)** | Round(s) in circular knitting |
| **dec(s)** | Decrease(s) | | **RS** | Right side |
| **dpn** | Double-pointed needle | | **sl** | Slip(ed) (ping). Slip stitches from left hand needle to right hand needle |
| **est** | Established | | | |
| **inc (s)** | Increase(s) | | **st(s)** | Stitch(es) |
| **k** | Knit | | **St st** | Stockinette stitch—k all RS rows, p all WS rows |
| **k2tog** | Knit two stitches together | | | |
| **MC** | Main color | | **tog** | Together |
| **p** | Purl | | **WS** | Wrong side |
| **p2tog** | Purl two stitches together | | | |
| **pat (s)** | Patterns(s) | | | |
| **psso** | Pass the slipped stitch over the last stitch worked | | | |

# Needle Conversions

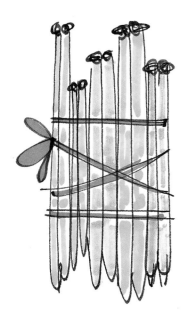

| Metric (mm) | US | Old UK |
|:---:|:---:|:---:|
| 2 | O | 14 |
| 2.25 | 1 | 13 |
| 2.5 | | |
| 2.75 | 2 | 12 |
| 3 | | |
| 3.25 | 3 | 10 |
| 3.5 | 4 | |
| 3.75 | 5 | |
| 4 | 6 | 8 |
| 4.5 | 7 | 7 |
| 5 | 8 | 6 |
| 5.5 | 9 | 5 |
| 6 | 10 | 4 |
| 6.5 | 10.5 | 3 |
| 7 | | 2 |
| 7.5 | | 1 |
| 8 | 11 | O |
| 9 | 13 | OO |
| 10 | 15 | OOO |

# Index